PLANTS

Written by
Andrew Charman

Illustrated by
Martine Collings, Charles Raymond
and John Shipperbottom

CONTENTS

2 Plants for life

Plants are the most extraordinary things, even the ordinary ones. All kinds of amazing plants have developed over millions of years. There are now plants that can grow hundreds of metres high, live on other plants, catch insects and look like stones.

Every part of our lives is affected by plants. We could not live without them. They feed us, heal us, clothe us, transport us, protect us, and they give us the air that we breathe.

All the amazing features they have and incredible ways they behave are to help them survive and grow.

The bee orchid has flowers that attract bee pollinators.

Stone plants look just like stones and, in this way, they escape being eaten.

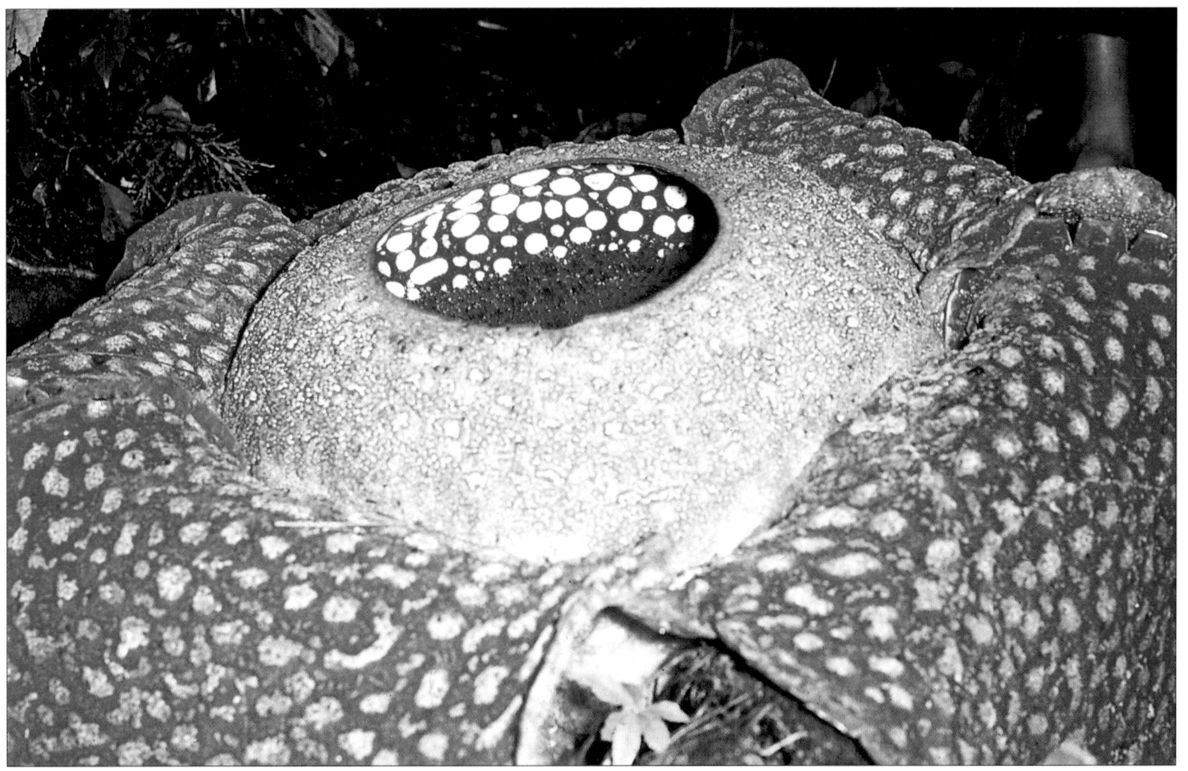

Rafflesia is the single biggest flower in the world. It is a parasite, taking its food from other plants.

Buttress roots may help to stop very tall rain forest trees from falling over.

A world of plants

Earth is a planet covered with plants. It is possible to put plants into a small number of very broad groups. To sort plants, you have to know how they are made, how they live and whether or not they produce seeds. Here are the main groups:

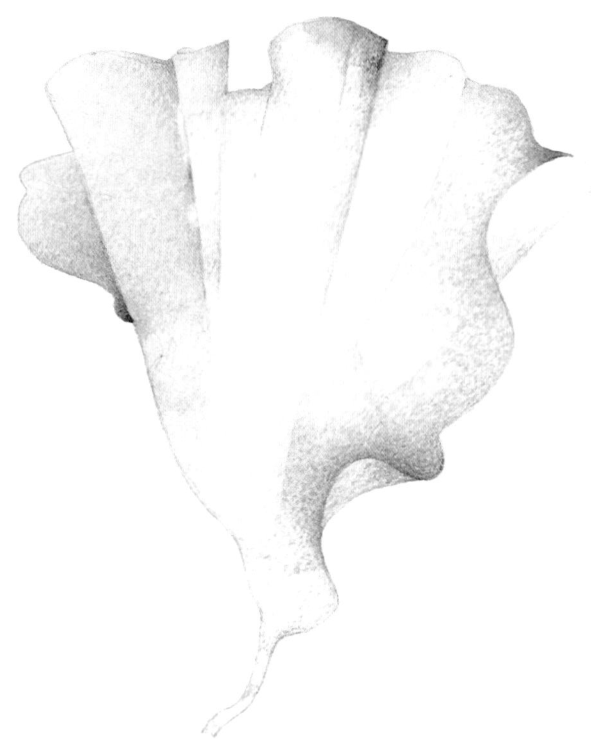

Sea lettuce is a kind of alga.

Algae

Seaweeds, which we we usually see on the beach, are kinds of algae. The green scum which forms on fish tanks, and the greenish-grey powder on tree bark, are also kinds of algae. Algae do not produce seeds.

Fungi

The mushrooms and toadstools which we see in damp places in the autumn are fungi. They do not produce seeds. The part we see carries spores. These spores will be blown away in the air and eventually grow into new fungi. Yeast (used in baking) and moulds are also kinds of fungi.

The penny bun fungus – a type of fungi

Lichen

The orange or grey crust we often see on bricks, stones or logs is called lichen. There are thousands of different kinds of lichens and they are all made in a very unusual way. They are made up of two very different kinds of plant: a fungi and an alga. The alga makes the food from water, air and sunlight (see page 8), while the fungi gets food from whatever the lichen is growing on. The fungi also attaches the lichen to the rock or log. Again, lichen do not produce seeds.

Lichen growing on a stone

Ferns

Ferns are often found in damp, shady places, although some will grow in dry areas. Horsetails and club mosses are related to ferns. They all reproduce with spores.

Bracken fern

Mosses and liverworts

These small plants tend to grow in wet and humid places – in bogs and beside streams. Like ferns, they do not produce flowers or seeds, but spores.

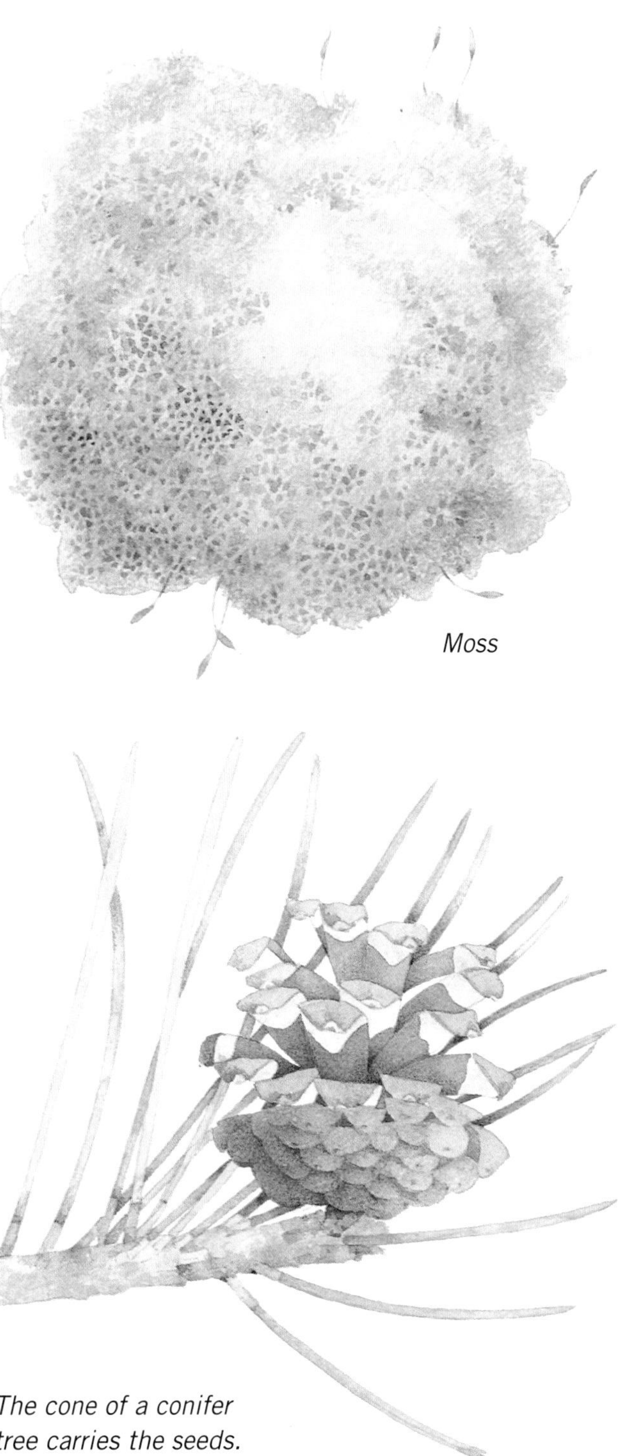

Moss

The cone of a conifer tree carries the seeds.

Seed plants

These plants reproduce with seeds. There are two groups of seed plants. One group, which includes conifer trees, have seeds which are not protected. The other group, the flowering plants, have seeds that are protected by a tough outer coating. Flowering plants are the most successful plants (see pages 6–7). There are nearly a quarter of a million different kinds.

Words to remember

Spores – tiny packages of cells that can grow into new plants.

The parts of a plant

No two kinds, or species, of plant are exactly alike. This is because they have developed different ways of surviving. Some may be tall, such as sunflowers; others, like daisies, can be short. Although they are different, their parts do roughly the same jobs.

The root

The root holds the plant in the ground and keeps it upright. The end of the root is continually growing and pushing its way between the particles of soil. Tiny root hairs absorb water and mineral salts from the soil. At the tip of the root is a hard cap which protects it from being worn away. Some plants have roots that can store food.

The stem

The stem holds up the plant so that its leaves catch as much of the sunlight as they can. It also connects the roots to the leaves.

At the top of the stem, this plant (opposite) has brightly coloured and scented flowers to attract insects. These insects carry out pollination (see page 12). This must happen if the plant is to produce seeds.

Leaves

The leaves take in light from the sun, carbon dioxide gas from the air, and water from the soil to produce food (see page 8). The upper surface of the leaf has a waterproof layer. This stops the leaf from losing too much water. On the under surface are pores (tiny holes) which control the gases going in and out, and how much water is lost.

Cells

All living things are made up of cells. Some plants consist of only one or a small number of cells. Most plants are made up of millions of cells. Cells can become specialized to do one particular job, such as carrying water or making food. To do this, the same kind of cells join together to form tissues.

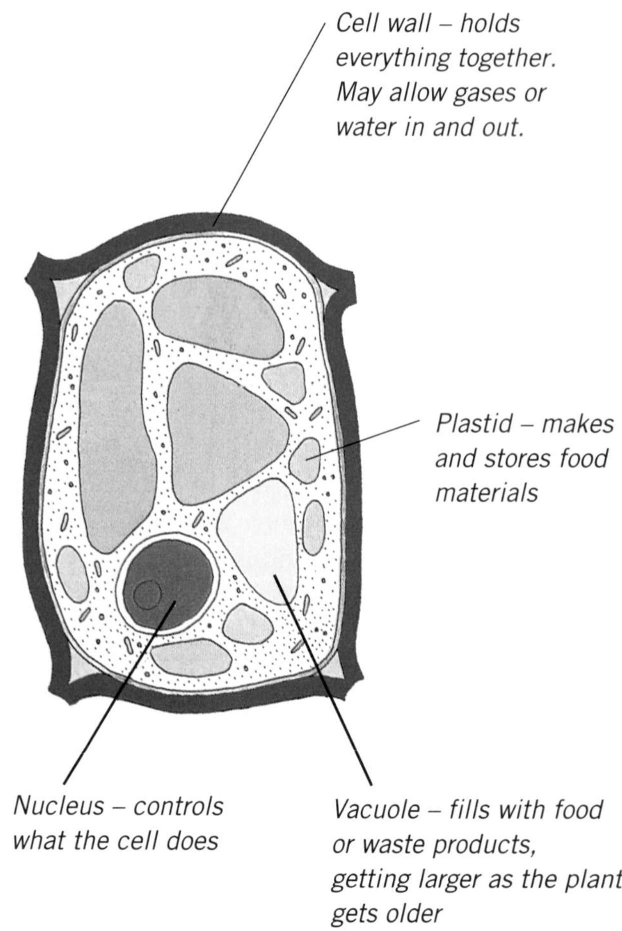

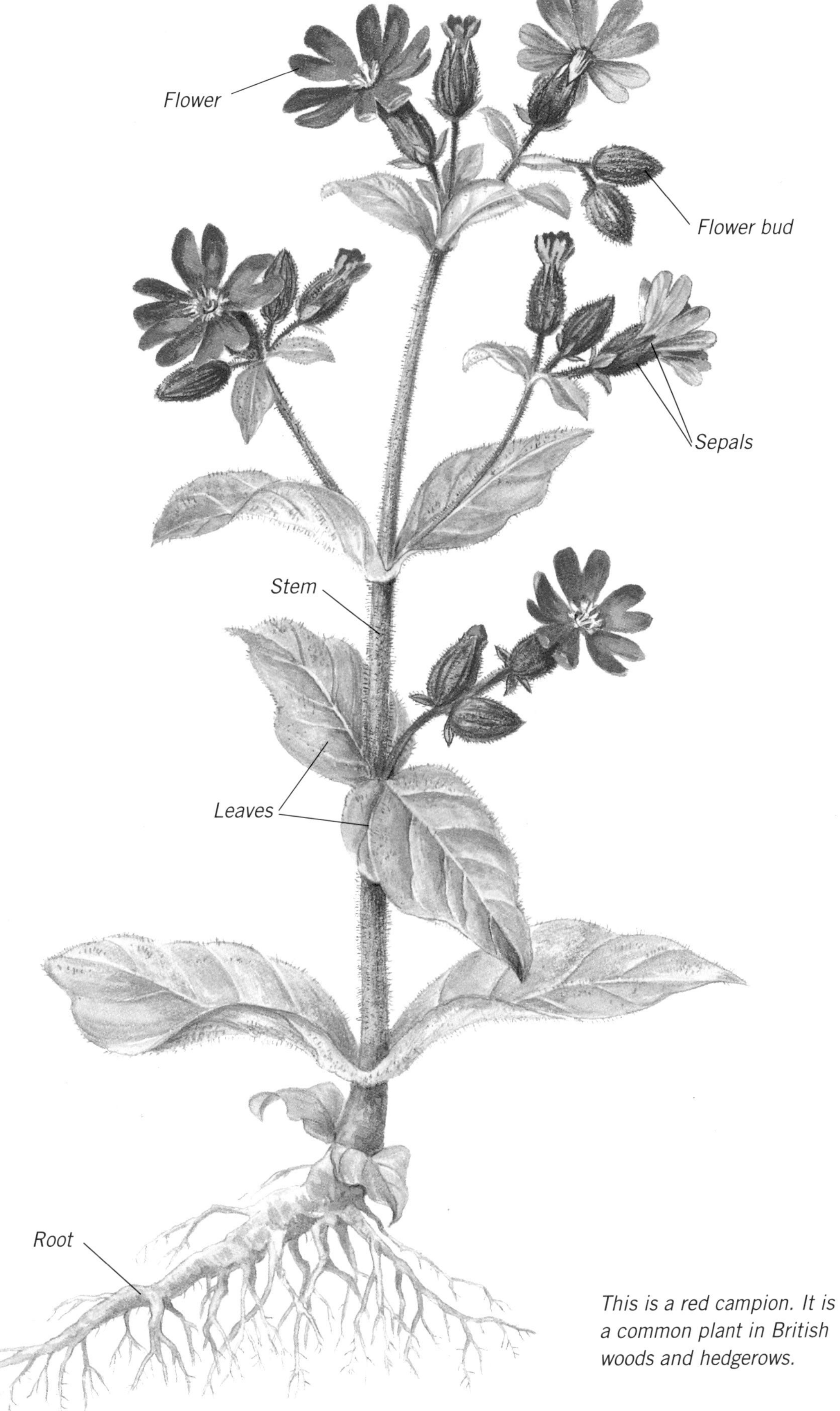

This is a red campion. It is a common plant in British woods and hedgerows.

How plants feed

Plants don't look as if they do much, but all day long they are growing and reacting to their environment. The most important thing they do is make their own food. This is called photosynthesis.

Making food

Plants make their food from carbon dioxide and water, using light from the sun. Carbon dioxide from the air, and water from the soil pass into the leaves. When light falls on to the leaves, the gas and the water join together to make glucose. This is the plant's food which helps it to grow. Oxygen is given off by the plant at the same time (see page 46).

The need for healthy soil

To stay healthy, plants also need mineral salts from the soil such as calcium, magnesium, phosphorus and copper.

If the soil does not have enough of these minerals, the plants will not grow properly. We can give plants more minerals by adding fertilizers to the soil (see page 43).

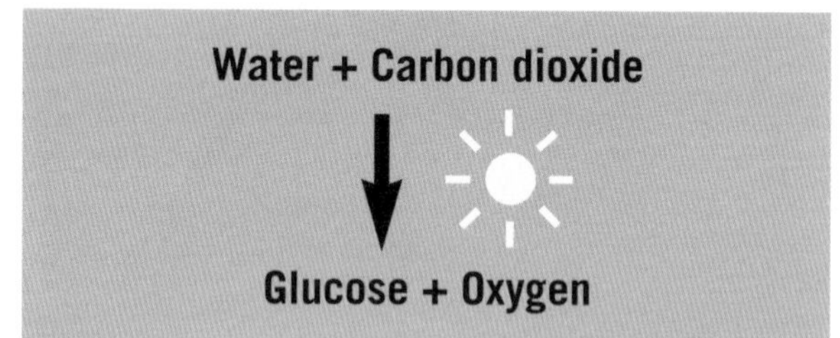

Plants and water

Plants need water for photosynthesis. Water also helps them to stay firm – without it, they droop. Water dries, or evaporates, from pores (tiny holes) in the leaves. This water is replaced by more coming up from the roots.

A plant makes its food from carbon dioxide and water when sunlight falls on to its leaves.

Death-trap plants

Some plants have an even more unusual way of getting extra food – they eat insects. The Venus' fly-trap and the pitcher plant are good examples. These plants have special ways of catching unwary insects. The victim is trapped and digested, and the nutrients that make up its body are taken in by the plant.

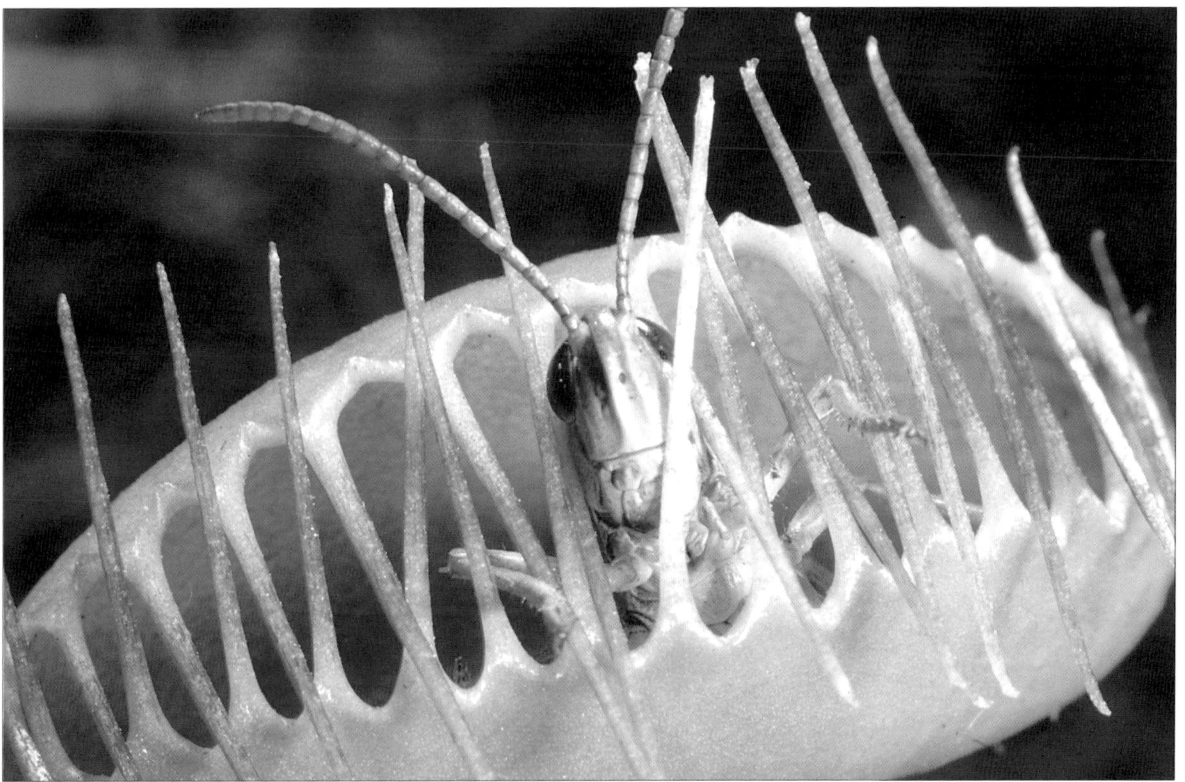

The Venus' fly-trap catches insects in two jaw-like structures. The spines along the outside edges stop the victim from escaping before the jaws are tightly shut.

Taking from others

There are some plants that do not photosynthesise. They live on and get their food from other plants. These are called parasitic plants. Toothwort gets its food from the roots of the hazel tree. Only its flowers appear above the ground. A dodder plant twines itself around the stem of another plant to take food from it.

Common dodder smothering another plant

Growing and changing

Plants change as the year passes. They grow larger every day. Flowers bloom and die, and seeds are produced. Different seasons affect them too.

Growing

Unlike animals, plants keep growing throughout their lives. This growth not only makes them bigger, but it also enables them to move. Plants grow towards the light (see page 8).

Plants grow in height and their stems get thicker. At the growing tip of the shoot, the cells (see page 6) divide into two identical cells. These new cells then start to grow – they may get 1000 times bigger. This is what makes a shoot grow so quickly.

Growing wood

Trees and bushes grow woody stems. In the stem is a thin layer of tissue, called the cambium, which produces new cells. This makes the trunk get thicker.

Opening for the sun

Growing is not the only way plants react to outside conditions. Some, such as dandelions, open their flowers when the sun shines and close them when it does not.

Different life cycles

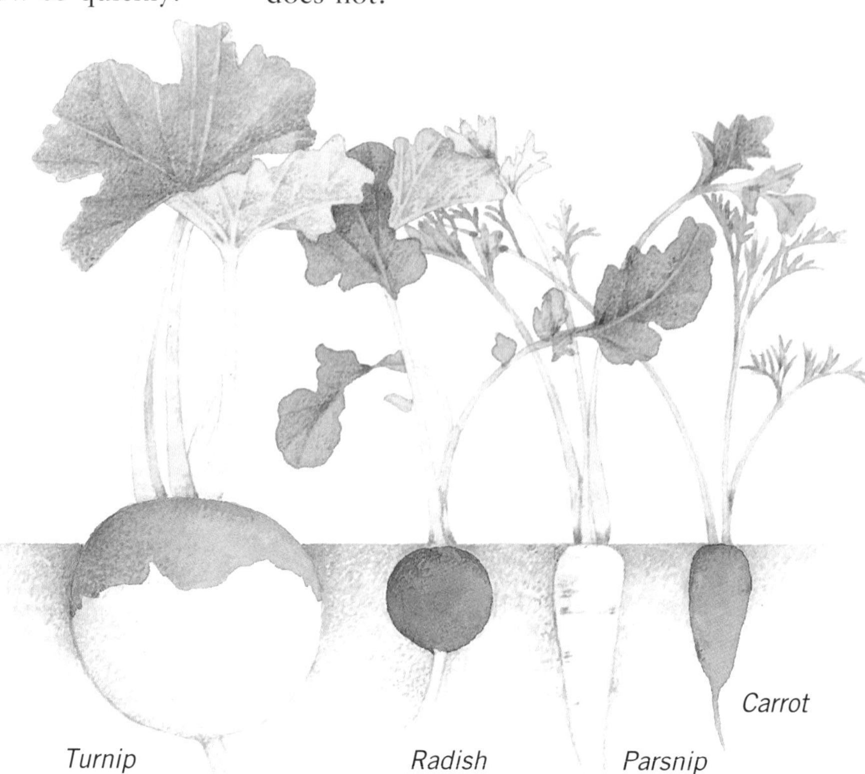

Turnip, radish, parsnip and carrot. These plants are biennials; the root vegetables are their food stores.

Plants live for different lengths of time. Annuals, such as peas and beans, take one year to complete their cycle. Biennials take two years. Carrots are a good example of this. The plant grows quickly in the first year and produces a store of food in the form of a big root – the carrot. We can pull up and eat this food store at the end of its first year. This store would be used to grow flowers and seeds the following year. Perennials live for three years or more. These include trees and shrubs.

Changing with the seasons

In the winter, it is too cold and dark for many plants to survive. Annuals die and their seeds wait for spring to come. Biennials lose their outer stems and leaves. Below ground, their bulbs or roots produce new shoots in the spring. Deciduous trees (see page 31) are perennials. They live for many years. In the autumn, they lose their leaves. They pass the winter as woody skeletons. In the spring, the temperature rises and there is more daylight. New leaves begin to grow because the tree can now take water from the ground which may have been frozen.

Spring

Summer

Autumn

Winter

An oak tree looks different during the four seasons of the year.

Plants and pollen

Just like animals, plants produce young. In flowering plants, male cells are transferred from one plant to the female cells in another. This second plant is now ready to produce seeds – it has been fertilized. These seeds will grow into new plants.

Stigma
Style
(female part)
Anther
Filament
Stamen (male part)
Petal
Ovary
Ovule
Sepals – there are several of these and they protect the flower when in bud.

What is a flower?

There are many different kinds of flowers. They all have basically the same parts. The male parts and the female parts are usually found on the same flower. Some plants produce separate male and female flowers; other plants are themselves either male or female.

Insects and pollen

The colourful petals and sweet scent of flowers attract insects and other animals. These animals transfer the male cells, the pollen, to the female cells.

As well as colour and scent, some flowers also make sugary nectar. The insect visits the flower to feed on the nectar. As it feeds, it brushes against the anthers and pollen sticks to its body. It then visits another flower and some of the pollen is brushed off on to that flower's stigma. Fertilization can only happen if both plants are of the same species.

As the honey bee crawls about on the flower feeding on the nectar, its body is dusted with pollen.

Different kinds of flowers

For millions of years, plants have been developing different kinds of flowers to attract the insects' attention. Flowers may occur on their own or in groups. Plants have developed some special tricks to attract insects. Flowers that open at night to attract moths are pale in colour to reflect as much light as possible. Some flowers have lines of colour which guide the insects to the nectar.

From left to right: mullein, hogweed, wood meadowgrass and bindweed

> **Words to remember**
> Fertilization – the stage at which male and female cells join together.

Some plants attract just one kind of insect. The insect and the plant need each other to survive. Bats, small mammals and birds also carry out the pollination for some species of plants.

For some plants, an amazing trick is to look like the insect. The flowers of bee orchids, for instance, look like bees. A bee flies in and tries to mate with the flower. As a result, its body is dusted with pollen.

Using the wind

Most trees and all grasses are wind-pollinated. They produce huge quantities of pollen in the hope that some of it will reach the stigmas of other plants. As they do not need to attract insects, the flowers are small and dull. The stigmas are large for catching pollen.

Plants and animals

Plants do not live alone. They are part of communities made up of many different plants and animals. In any one place, the living things depend on each other for their survival.

Living together

Living things depend on each other and their environment for food, shelter and protection. A woodland may be home to thousands of different kinds of living things. No two live exactly the same way, and they all depend on each other. The birds need the trees and shrubs in which they build their nests. The flowers need the insects for pollination. The trees rely on animals to help spread their seeds. This means there is a 'web' of relationships between plants and animals. The study of plants and animals living together in the environment is called ecology.

Food chains

In a food chain, one living thing depends on another living thing for its food. For example, at the bottom of the food chain (shown opposite) are the plants. There are animals such as small fish which eat them. These animals are, in turn, eaten by other animals. As you go up the chain, the number of animals gets smaller. At the end of the chain are the the top predators; no one eats them.

What affects one part of the chain can affect other parts. For example, if you pollute the water, the fish will die and this will result in fewer herons.

Moving on to the land

Land can be stripped of all its plants. It can be damaged by pollution or covered by molten lava. If it is then left alone, the plants will eventually come back. The first to arrive will be algae, lichens and mosses (see pages 4 and 5). Other plants come in stages, each one becoming longer-lasting than the ones before it. Eventually, trees and shrubs will return. A woodland may take a hundred years to grow back.

Foxgloves are among the first plants to move on to a bare patch of ground.

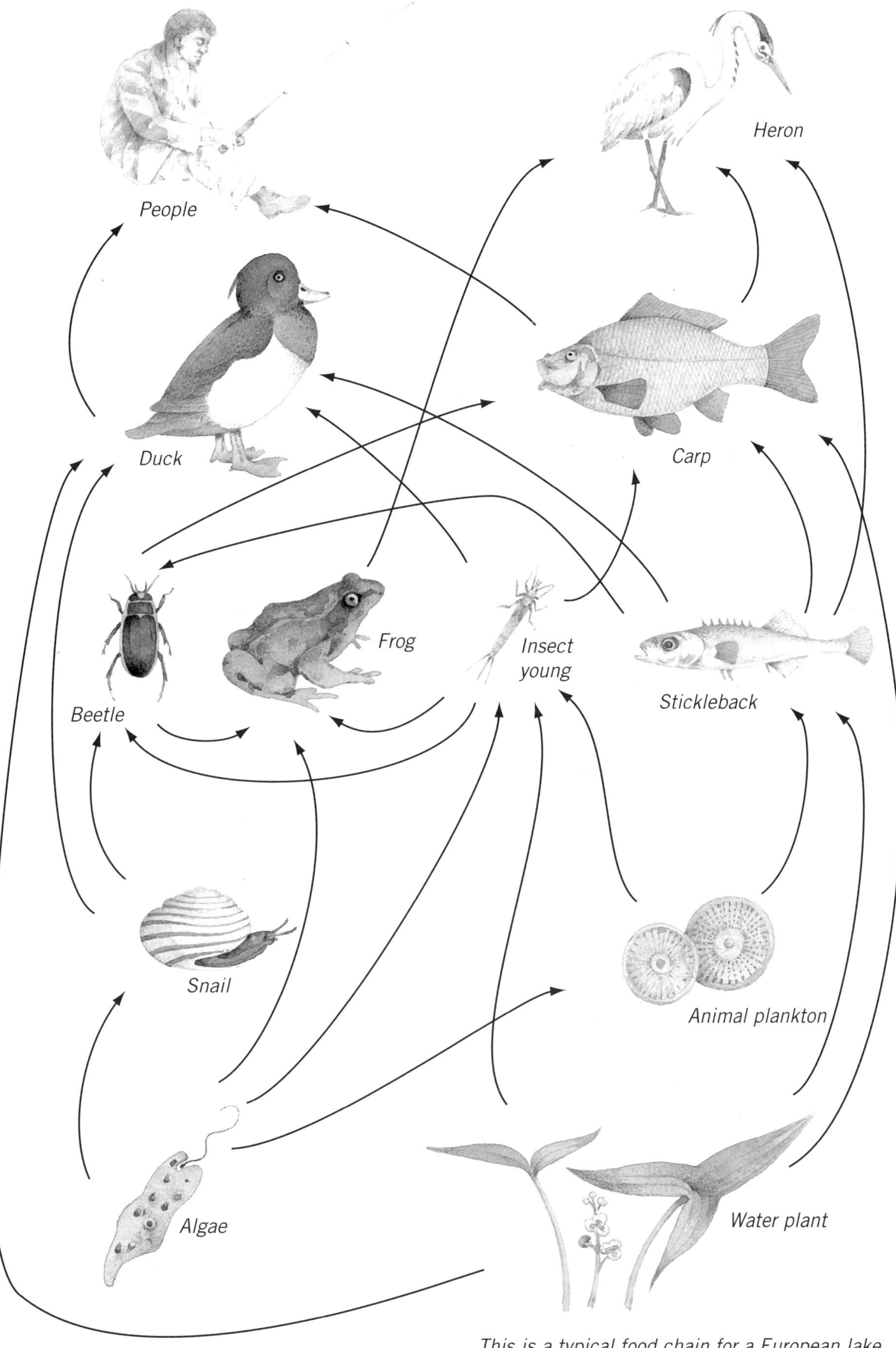

This is a typical food chain for a European lake. It shows what eats what.

Making and spreading seeds

In flowering plants, seeds are formed when the plant has been fertilized (see page 13). New plants can grow from these seeds. Seeds can be very different shapes and sizes. They have many ways of moving away from the parent plant. This movement is called seed dispersal.

The fruit and the seed

After fertilization, the female parts of the flower (ovary) become the fruit. The ovule inside the ovary (see page 12) becomes the seed. The seed has parts which will become the root, stem and first leaves. The seed is protected by a tough outer coating, called the testa.

It is not always easy to tell which bit is the fruit and which the seed. With peas, for example, the peas are the seeds and the pea pod is the fruit. There may be just one seed, as with plums, several as with peas, or thousands as have been counted in poppy capsules.

Burdocks have seeds with spikes that stick to animals' fur.

Scattering seeds

Over millions of years, plants have developed many different ways of scattering their seeds. Plants use wind, water and animals to spread their seeds; some burst open and scatter their seeds around them. Whether those seeds will germinate or not depends on the conditions they find.

In dandelions, it is the ring of sepals around each flower that becomes the parachute. These fly away in the wind, each carrying a single seed.

Different fruits

There are many different kinds of fruits. They all have the same job – to be attractive and tasty to birds and animals. The fruit is eaten, but the seeds pass through the animal without being digested. The seeds may be lucky enough to land somewhere where they can grow.

Plum

Plums are formed from a single ovary. The skin, flesh and hard 'nut' are the fruit. Inside the nut is the true seed.

Fig

Figs are formed from many ovaries of several flowers growing together as one unit.

Raspberries

These fruits are formed from about ten or twelve ovaries belonging to a single flower. Blackberries are the same.

Words to remember

Germination – early stages in the growth of a seed or spore.

Seeds starting life

With luck, some of the seeds produced by the plant will drop on to a patch of ground where they can grow, or germinate (see page 17). This patch will have nutrients, light and water. Even then, the seeds may not germinate immediately.

Sleeping seeds

The seeds may lie dormant (do nothing) for a while. In countries with warm summers and cold winters, like Britain, many plants release their seeds at the end of the summer. If the seeds germinated then, the seedlings would have to face a cold winter. So they wait, and grow in the spring when it is warmer and there are more hours of daylight.

Holding back the seeds

Many seeds contain a chemical which stops them from germinating immediately. This chemical is washed out of the seed by rain. This takes time – the time it takes for winter to pass, for example. Other seeds have a tough outer coating which takes time to wear away.

Seeds staying alive

The length of time seeds can live without germinating varies. Willow and poplar seeds can only survive for a few days. 'Weeds', however, can sometimes live for forty years! The seeds of the sacred lotus can live for 120 years, but the record is probably held by an Arctic lupin. Seeds that are ten thousand years old have come to life when given warmth and light.

Seed leaves

There are two main types of flowering plants. Woody trees, shrubs and many garden plants are called **dicots**. These have two seed leaves in the seed. Grasses, palms and orchids belong to another group called **monocots**. They have only one seed leaf (see page 19).

The castern lotus is sacred to many people in India and Tropical Asia. It stands for purity, beauty, the sun and life.

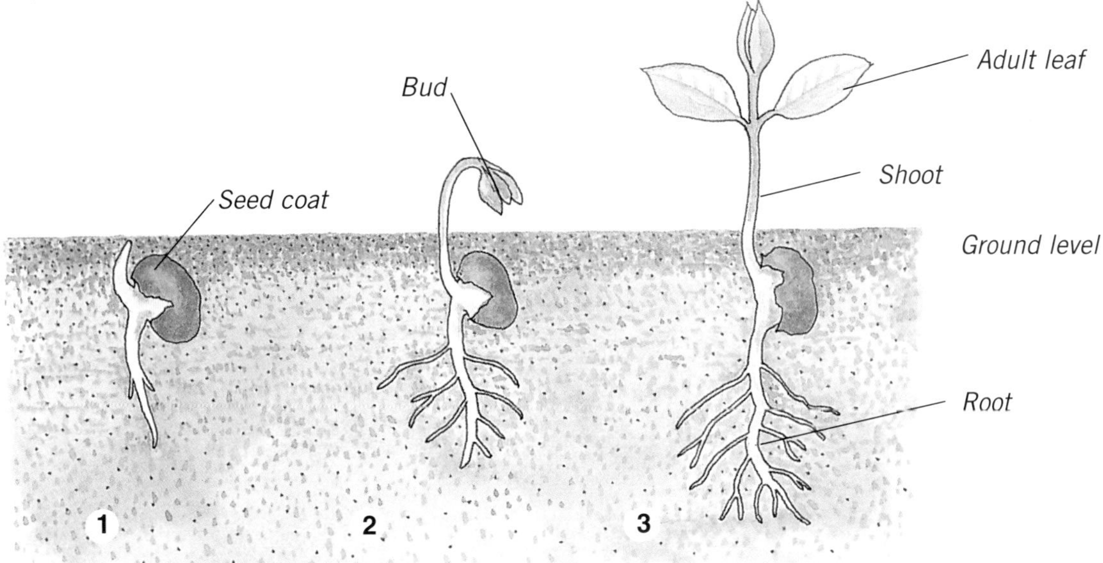

Growing

When conditions are right, the cells in the seed begin to divide and it grows.

1 The seed grows first at the root which breaks out of the seed coat. The root begins to take in water and mineral salts.

2 The shoot, or stem, often grows at first as a loop. This means that the delicate bud at the tip is not damaged as it pushes its way through the soil. Usually, the root grows downwards while the shoot seeks out the light.

3 The seed comes complete with seed leaves. In some plants, these stay below ground and provide food for the new growth. In others, they appear above ground and begin photosynthesis (see page 8). The seed leaves often do not look at all like the adult leaves that appear later. Once photosynthesis has begun, the seedling can feed itself and no longer depends on food from the seed.

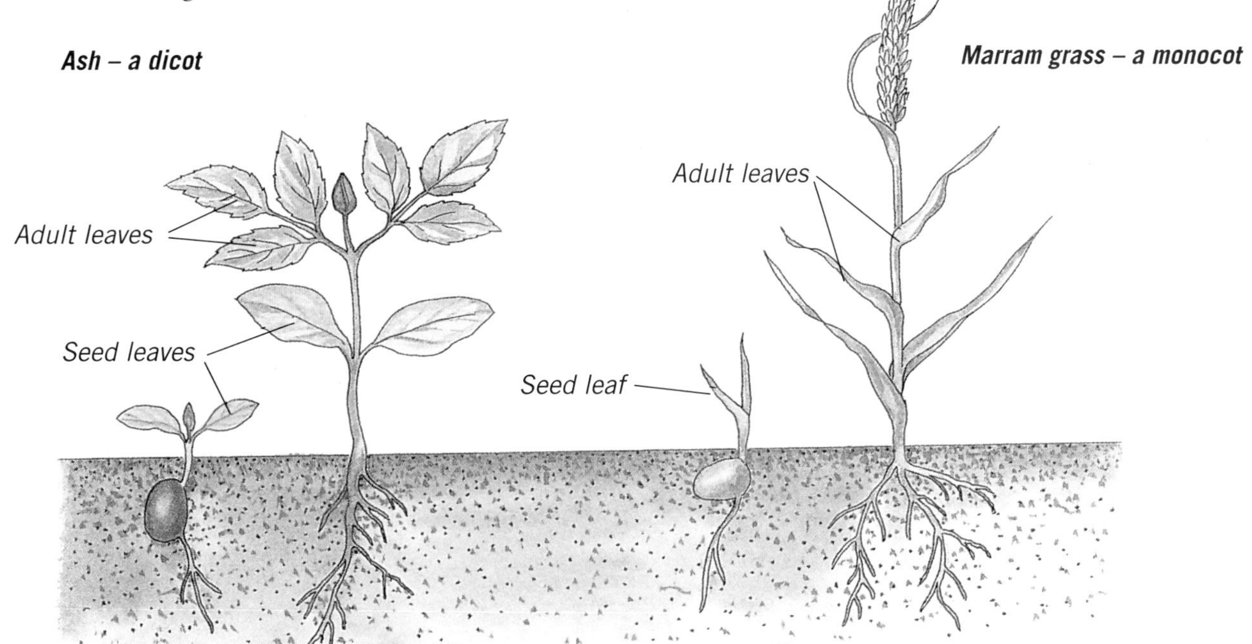

New life without seeds

Flowering plants have another way of reproducing themselves. This can take place without flowers and seeds. What happens is that part of the plant becomes a new plant. This is called vegetative reproduction.

Identical plants

Most flowering plants can use vegetative reproduction as well as flowers and seeds. Vegetative reproduction avoids pollination and germination, both of which are risky and may not happen. The problem with this method, is that the new plants are exactly the same as the parent. If conditions change and the parent dies, so do the new plants. If the new plants have been formed from a seed and are slightly different from the parent, they have a better chance of surviving.

Stem growth

Often the new growth comes from buds on the stem. Potatoes are known as stem tubers. They are a store of food and each potato can grow into a completely new plant. Some bulbs, such as crocus bulbs, reproduce themselves every year. If you break off the new bulbs and plant them, they will grow into new plants.

The house leek produces a ring of 'offsets' on stem runners. Each of the offsets can become a new plant.

After they have produced their fruit, strawberry plants grow leafy stems called runners. These run along the ground.

Branching out

Some new plants grow from buds on stems which stretch out along the surface of the soil or just below it. They are called runners. Strawberries and buttercups grow like this.

Rhizomes are stems that grow under the ground. Bindweed and couch grass grow like this. New plants grow up at certain points along the stem. Once the new plant has roots and leaves of its own it can grow without the parent plant.

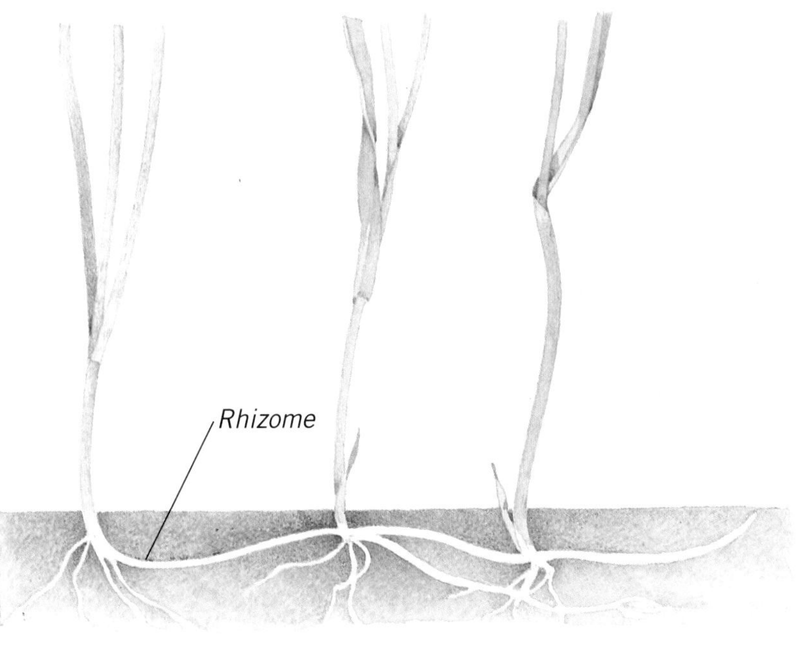

Vegetative reproduction makes couch grass a stubborn weed.

Plants worldwide

Plants live in almost every part of our planet. It is only in the hottest and coldest places that they cannot survive.

The vegetation zones

Which plants grow where in the world depends on the climate (weather patterns). This affects the temperature, the amount of light and water, and what the soil is like. Across the world, there are certain vegetation zones that we can easily identify. Particular plants have adapted to survive the conditions in each zone. Some live in only one zone, others are more widespread.

No two species of plant live in exactly the same way. Some plants like shade, some like wet soil – they are all different. Being different means that they do not all want the same things. This increases their chances of survival, and they do not need to compete with each other.

In each vegetation zone, there are certain plants that are dominant. They take most of the light, water and nutrients. Often these are the trees.

> **Words to remember**
> Temperate – places which have warm summers and cold or cool winters.

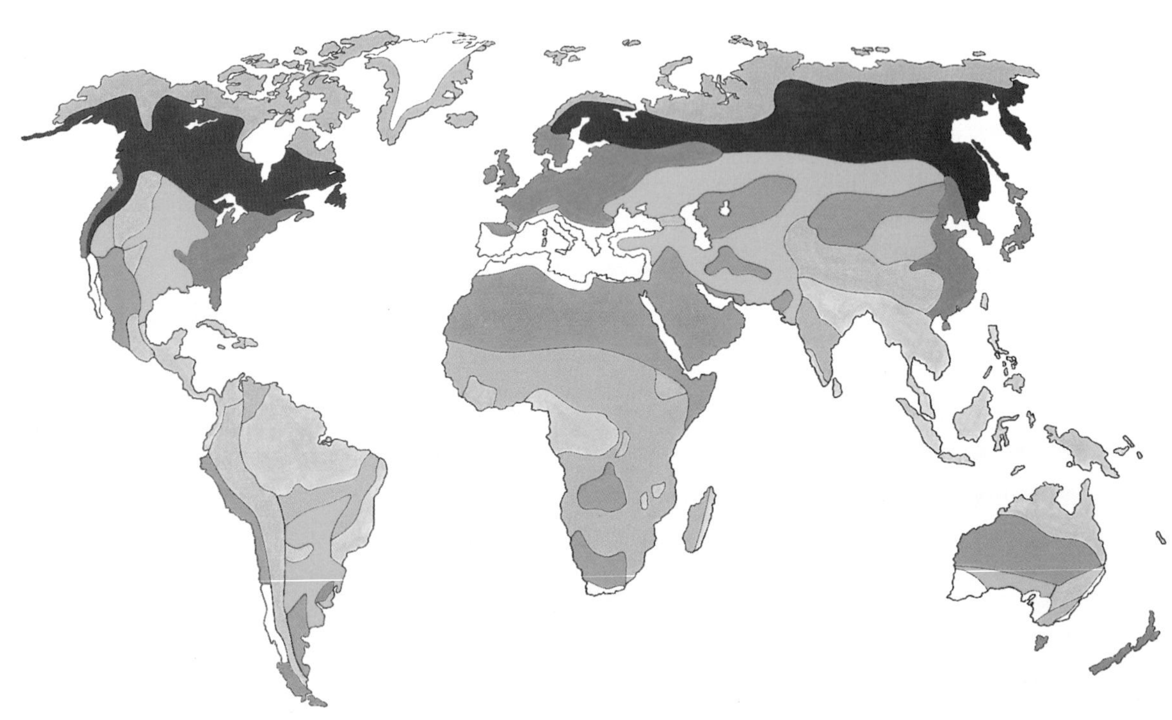

This map of the world shows where the different vegetation zones can be found. Use the key on page 23 to help you.

The open grasslands

There are two different kinds of grassland in the world – the savannah and the steppe. Savannah grasslands are found in dry, tropical areas in Africa, South America and Australia. In Africa, the grassland is lush in the rainy season and dry at other times. It is dotted with acacia trees which give shade to elephants and lions. The grass is grazed by huge herds of plant-eating animals such as wildebeest and zebra.

Steppe grassland is found in temperate areas of North America, Russia, South America and Australia. In America, it was once the home of wandering herds of bison. Large areas of these grasslands are now used for growing crops.

A herd of wildebeest on the African savannah.

Key

Hot deserts

Only plants that can survive great heat and very little water live in these zones.

Cold deserts

Ice

Here, it is too cold for plants to survive. The water is always frozen.

Tundra

It is cold, but there is a little water. There are short shrubs, mosses, grasses and some flowering plants.

Coniferous forests

The trees here are mostly evergreen with needle-like leaves (see page 30).

Temperate forests

These forests have great seasonal changes. Deciduous trees such as oak, birch and beech live here (see page 31).

Tropical rain forests

These are the lushest and most varied vegetation zones in the world.

Temperate grasslands

These are flat, sandy plains. Rain drains away quickly so that trees cannot grow.

Tropical grasslands

These are home to great herds of grazing animals. In places, the grass is mixed with thorny scrub or open woodland.

Scrub

Evergreen trees or shrubs, or open grassland.

Mountains

Mountains often have forests at their base, tundra-like plants higher up, and usually just rock, or ice and snow, at the top.

Plants in water

The sea is the largest habitat on Earth. It is home to millions of creatures. Just as on land, plants photosynthesize to make food.

The plants that use most of this light are tiny blue-green algae. They are then eaten by plant-eaters, such as krill, who are eaten by meat-eaters including whales and sharks. So plants are the source of all food in the sea.

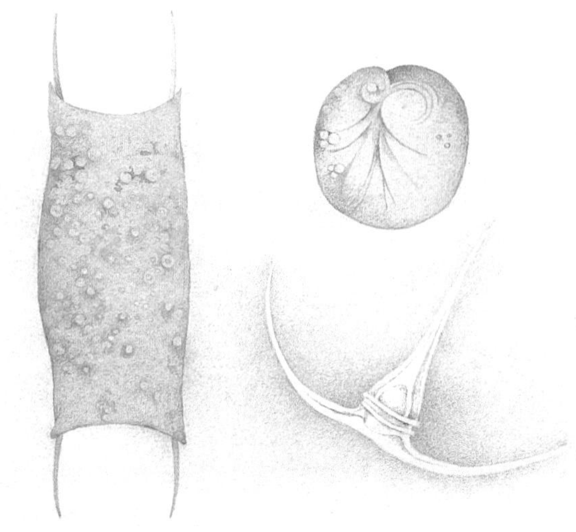

Tiny plants called phytoplankton drift in the surface layers of the sea where it is warm and the light can reach them.

Plants on the beach

The seaweeds that we see on the beach at low tide are also algae. They live on the edge of the sea where they are covered by water at high tide and exposed at low tide. They have tough outer layers to prevent them being dried out by the sun. Seaweeds have holdfasts (instead of roots) which fix them to the rocks. They are flexible plants and can bend with the water. They are not easily damaged.

A diver swimming through a kelp forest. Kelp is one of the largest seaweeds. It can grow to a length of 60 metres.

Further up the beach

Some land plants are able to live near the edge of the sea. They can grow where there is a lot of salt. Marram grass grows long, spreading roots which bind the sand. This stops the sand being washed or blown away, and eventually makes land for other plants to grow on.

The long roots of marram grass seek out water. They bind the loose sand so that it builds up into dunes.

Freshwater plants

Plants cannot take root in fast-moving rivers, but, as the current slows down, they can take a hold. Some river plants, such as fanwort, have fine leaves which are not damaged by the current. Many water plants have their roots in the soil at the bottom but show their flowers above the water. They can then be pollinated by insects. Water lilies use the surface of the water to support their huge leaves.

Words to remember

Habitat – the conditions in which a living thing lives.

The leaves of the Amazonian water lilies can reach a diameter of more than 2 metres. They are strengthened by strong ribs on the underside.

Life in the cold

In the world's cold places, there are sharp, icy winds. There is not very much rain and what does fall may come down as snow. Any water in the ground is likely to be frozen. Plants have found ways of surviving all this.

Mountain survivors

The higher you travel up a mountain, the colder the air becomes. Plants that live on high mountains are called alpine plants. They are usually small and compact, growing in thick clusters and flattened mats. This stops them from being damaged by cold winds. Their leaves are small which means they do not lose too much precious water.

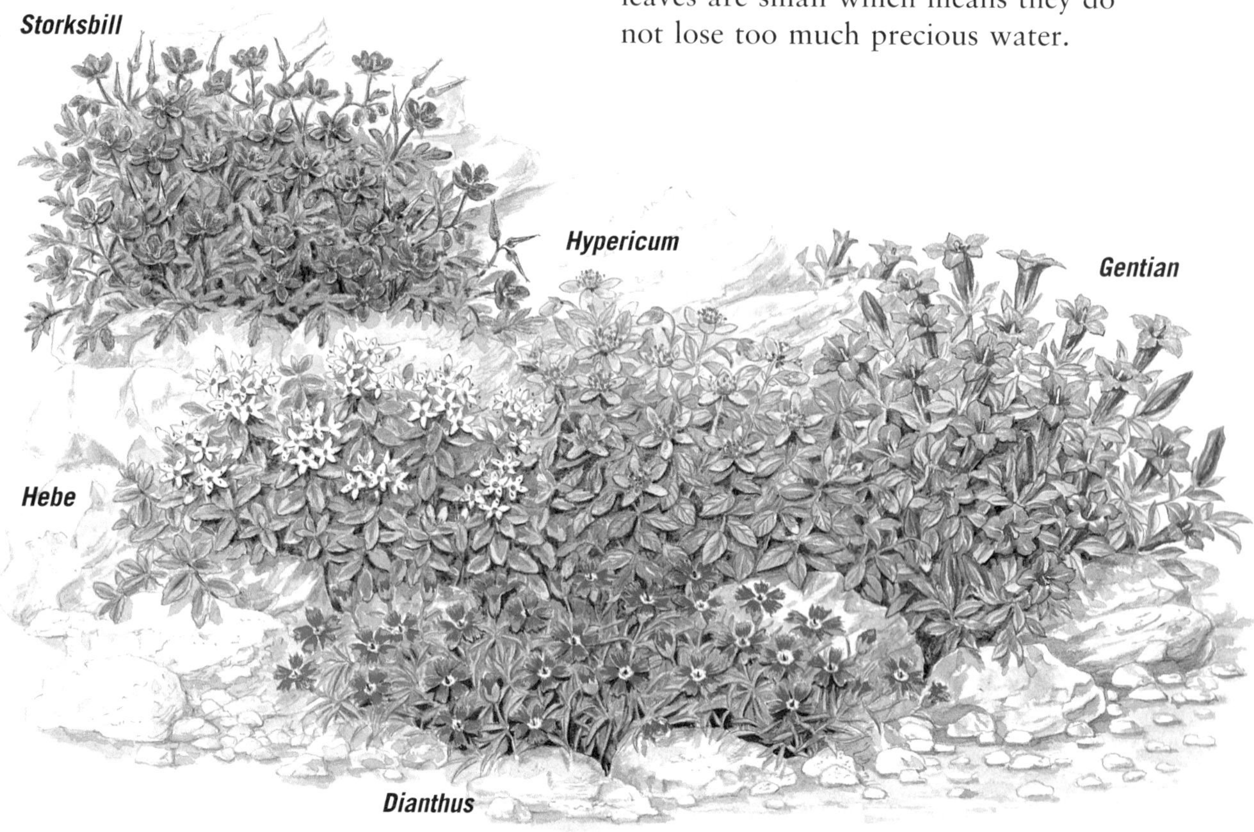

A collection of mountain, or alpine, plants.

The silversword grows on the mountains of Hawaii. Here, near the tropics, the sun is hotter and plants are exposed to dangerous ultraviolet rays. The silversword is protected from these rays by fine white hairs that grow on its leaves.

The dwarf hebe grows on mountains in New Zealand. It forms thick, low-lying cushions. These trap heat and prevent damage by the wind, especially water loss. The leaves are tough enough to withstand sharp frosts.

In the mountains of Central Africa and South America live plants of great size. Lobelias and groundsels grow several metres high. It is not known exactly why. In other parts of the world, these plants are quite small.

Life on the tundra

On the edge of the icy Arctic, around the North Pole, is an area known as the tundra. Roughly the same kind of plants grow here as in the alpine zone of mountains. The tundra land is covered with snow during the long, dark winters. When summer comes, a thin top layer of soil thaws out. Lichens, algae and mosses are able to grow. Also, there are a hundred species of flowering plants such as cranberries, stitchwort and dwarf birch. Trees cannot grow – it is too cold and there is not enough water. The Antarctic, around the South Pole, has few plants because it is too cold. Lichens grow on the rocks, and mosses grow where there is soil.

In some mountain areas, the summers are short and the winters long. The plants bloom quickly and at the same time.

Life in the heat

There are some large areas on Earth where very few plants can survive. These are the deserts. Here, there is very little water for the plants to use. The frozen expanses of the poles are deserts (see page 27). So, too, are the Earth's hot spots.

Desert survivors

Some plants have found ways of surviving in the hot deserts. Some, such as lichens, can simply live for a long time with very little water in their tissues. The creosote bush just shuts down in a drought. Its mature leaves drop off and its buds turn brown. They stop photosynthesizing. When the rain comes, they turn green again and life continues.

The creosote plant stops growing during long periods of drought. It comes to life again when the rain falls.

Searching for water

Keeping water in is useful; so is being able to absorb every last drop of what does fall. Many desert plants have shallow roots that spread out over a very large area. Others send down deep roots to reach water.

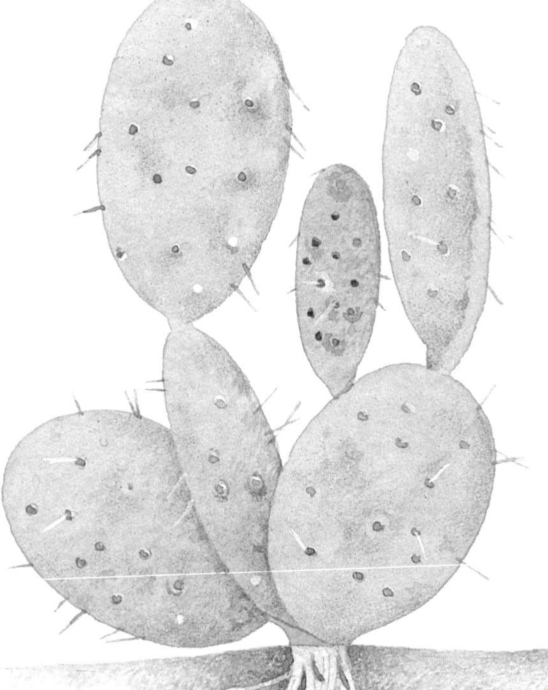

Cactus' roots do not go very deep. They spread out over a wide area to collect as much rain as possible. This is a prickly pear cactus.

Keeping the water in

Plants lose water through the pores (tiny holes) in their leaves. Water also evaporates from the surface. Most desert plants have their pores on the underside of the leaves to reduce this loss. Other plants have very small leaves or none at all and use the stem to carry out photosynthesis (see page 8).

The cactus' spines may protect the plant from the extremes of hot and cold and from attack by animals.

Storing water

Cacti are plants that can store water (succulents). They use their thick stems as containers. They have no leaves but lots of spines instead. This means that the plant does not have broad, flat areas that can be dried up in the sun.

Water in leaves

Some succulents, such as the necklace vine, use their leaves for storing water. Others use their roots. Leaf succulents live in slightly damper areas than those in which cacti can survive. Their leaves have a thick, waxy surface which protects them from the harsh sun and helps them to stay cool.

Blooming quickly

Some desert plants survive the long periods between rain storms not as plants, but as seeds. They may lay dormant, doing nothing for years. When the rain comes they bloom, are pollinated and set seed very quickly before the soil dries up again. There may be as many as 25 000 seeds per square metre just waiting for rain.

During periods of drought, a leaf succulent's leaves become shrivelled and wrinkly. They swell up with stored water when the rains come. This plant grows in Southern Africa.

Forests

Forests are communities of plants – the dominant plants are trees. Where light falls between the trees, smaller plants can survive. Some can even live on the trees themselves.

What is a tree?

A tree is a plant with a single woody stem. It is a material called lignin which makes the stem hard and strong. This enables trees to grow taller than other plants in the contest for light. The most common trees are the broadleaves, such as oak and ash; and the conifers, which include firs and spruces.

Coniferous forests

The northern parts of Europe, North America and Asia have coniferous forests. Spruces, firs, pines and cedars are the most common trees. They are evergreen – they do not lose all their leaves at once in autumn. These trees can survive in places where the winters are long, cold and dark. Their leaves are tough, leathery and needle-like and do not dry out in the cold winds.

In sunny gaps, shrubby plants such as bilberries and junipers survive. Grasses and plants such as wild strawberry can also be found. Mosses and lichens grow on the trees, and fungi live on the forest floor.

Coniferous trees cast a dense shade. Only when a tree dies and leaves a gap can other plants thrive on the forest floor.

Temperate forests

In more southerly parts of Europe, North America and Asia, there are temperate forests. Here, the summers are warm and the winters are cold. Broadleaved trees, such as oak, ash, beech, maple and birch grow in these forests. During the summer, the trees have leaves which cast a dense shade. In the autumn, they lose their leaves and lie dormant over the winter. These are called deciduous trees.

In the early spring, the trees do not have any leaves and there is less shadow. Many smaller plants grow in the light that falls on them. These include wood anemones, wild strawberries, primroses and bluebells.

Key

① *wild strawberries*
② *toadstools on moss*
③ *bilberries*
④ *chickweed*
⑤ *cowberries*
⑥ *Scots pines*
⑦ *juniper*
⑧ *Lady's tresses*
⑨ *fungus*
⑩ *lichen*

This is a rain forest in Venezuela, South America. Rain forest trees are evergreen, losing a few leaves throughout the year rather than all at once.

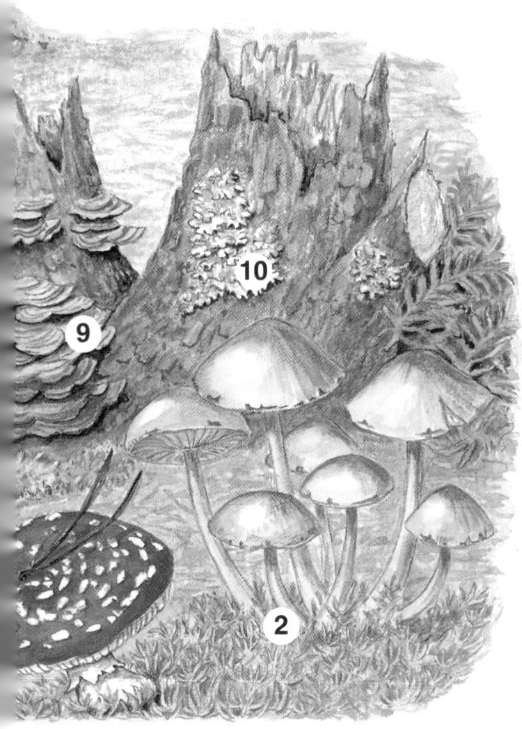

The crowded rain forests

The tropical rain forests are packed with plant life. Conditions are right for growth all year round: heavy rainfall, warm temperatures and long hours of daylight. The trees cast a dense shade with their dark green, glossy leaves. Taller trees break free of the shade, and below them thrive a wide variety of shrubs and smaller plants. Some plants grow on the trees themselves. These include lichens, mosses, liverworts, ferns and orchids. The trees are entwined with woody-stemmed climbing plants called lianas. These have their roots in the soil and develop a huge spread of leaves.

Plant defences

Most plants are rooted to the spot. Unlike animals, they cannot run away from their enemies. Fortunately, plants have different ways of defending themselves, such as fine hairs, stings or stabbing thorns.

Once stung, twice shy

Stinging nettles can be found in hedgerows and rough patches of ground. The stings of the stinging nettle are like tiny syringes. They are strengthened by a glass-like material called silica. When an animal brushes against the plant, the stings pierce the skin. They inject a chemical which causes a painful rash.

Hairy plants

Insects crawl on to plants and suck nutrients out of the stems; some chew great holes in the leaves. The leaves of some plants are covered with fine hairs. Small insects find it difficult to walk across the surface, and so they give up and go elsewhere.

A stinging nettle sting enlarged many times.

Stinging nettles grow where the soil is rich in nutrients.

Ants to the rescue

Some acacia trees have ants to protect them. The ants live on the tree, feeding on the sweet-tasting pith (flesh) inside the thorns and on the leaves. In return for this food and shelter, the ants attack any animal that attempts to eat the leaves.

Dangerous chemicals

Many plants have substances in their leaves and stems which make them unpleasant or dangerous to eat. These dangerous chemicals have been used to make poisons. The South American Indians hunt with a poison called curare. This poison is now used in a safe form by surgeons to relax patients' muscles.

Indians from Ecuador make the curare poison from the bark of a vine.

Thistles protect themselves with prickles, which can be very painful if you try to pull one up without wearing thick gloves!

Spine attack

Spines, thorns and prickles are common forms of self-defence for plants. Briars and wild roses have sharp thorns on their stems which can be very painful to an animal or person.

A watery trap

Troublesome snails and insects can drown trying to get to the leaves of the plant called teasel. Where the pairs of leaves join the stem of the plant there is a pool of water. Insects trying to get to the leaves run the risk of a watery grave.

Food for all

Plants have been used for food and flavourings since the first people felt pangs of hunger. Over 10 000 different kinds have been eaten at one time or another, including fungi and seaweed.

Staple foods

Today, only a small number of crops provide the world with most of its food. These include rice, wheat, maize, barley and sugar cane. They are the world's most important crops and are known as the staples. Which crop is grown where depends on the climate. Rice is grown in tropical countries. Wheat is more common in cooler countries, such as Britain.

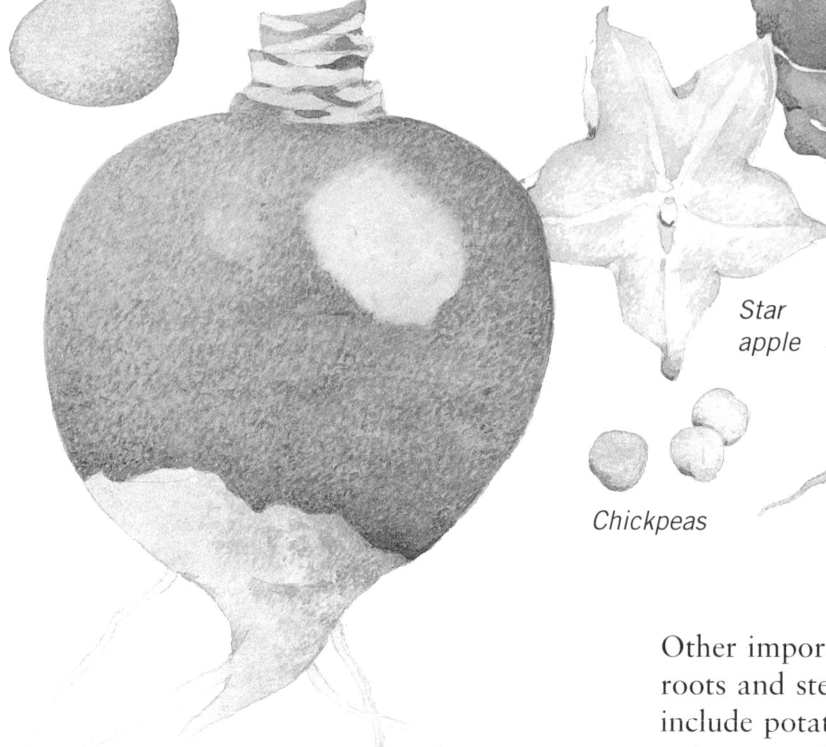

The many kinds of plant food we eat come from different parts of the plants. There are stems, leaves, seeds, fruits, even flowers.

Other important crops are the swollen roots and stems of many plants. These include potatoes, cassava, carrots, swedes, onions, turnips and many others.

When we eat pulses, we are enjoying the edible seeds of the pea family. Soya beans, lentils and chickpeas are all kinds of pulses. These are good sources of protein.

We also harvest the fruits of many plants including grapes, bananas, pineapples, tomatoes, oranges and apples. We eat the green leaves of cabbages and spinach, and the unopened flower heads of broccoli.

Oils from plants are also used in cooking. Oil crops come from olives, the oil palm, sunflowers, sesame seeds and coconuts.

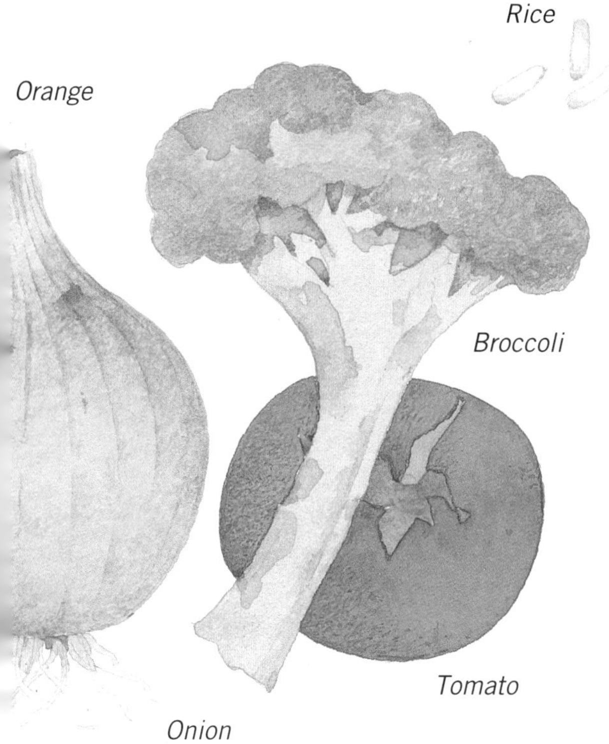

Old crops and new crops

For thousands of years, farmers have been improving their crops by only planting the seeds from their best plants. We now have crops that produce more food than ever before. It is hoped that these crops can help with food shortages across the world. Unfortunately these 'megacrops' can easily be attacked by disease and they need expensive fertilizers, machines and lots of water to grow.

Another future for plants

Some people believe that there is another way forward. This is to grow plants that can survive in harsh conditions. There are many such plants flourishing in the wild. Some like dry weather, others succeed in soil which is too salty for other crops. For example, the buffalo gourd grows in the very dry parts of Mexico and parts of America. It can be 3–4 metres long, and its fruits produce seeds with lots of protein and oil.

Jackfruit plants grow well in salty soils. The fruits can be boiled, roasted or eaten fresh. This one is from Southern India.

The luxuries of life

There are a large number of plants that give us our luxuries. They make up the drinks we enjoy; the herbs and spices that add variety to our diets; the perfumes, cosmetics, shampoos and bath oils we use to make ourselves clean or just more attractive.

Plants we drink

Probably the most important plants we use as drinks are tea and coffee. Both have been enjoyed for thousands of years. Tea is made from the fresh young leaves of a plant which is grown in hot countries, particularly India. Coffee is made from the roasted beans (seeds) of a tropical evergreen shrub. Both tea and coffee are grown on large plantations.

Chocolate is made from the beans of the cocoa plant. It was first used by the Aztecs of Central America.

All kinds of alcoholic drinks are made from plants. Barley, rice, grapes, molasses, and even potatoes, are commonly used. They are flavoured with hops, juniper berries, aniseed and many other plants.

Flavouring food

Herbs have leaves with pleasant flavours – they add interest to food. In medieval times, before refrigeration, they were used to disguise the flavour of rotting food. They came originally from Europe. Among them are thyme, rosemary, basil, marjoram and oregano – they are all members of the mint family.

Spices come from tropical woody plants. Many are the seeds of trees. Cinnamon comes from the bark of a tree; vanilla comes from the seeds of a climbing orchid. Nutmeg and mace come from the same tree – nutmeg from the seeds, mace from the fleshy part of the fruit.

Plants for make-up

All over the world people use make-up to enhance their looks. Modern make-ups are rarely made entirely from plants, but some people do still use natural make-up. The Amazonian Indians make one from the waxy coating of the seeds of a tree. The seeds are made into a red paste – deep scarlet for the men, a paler orange for the women. The indians like to wear bright make-up because they hate drabness – it makes them think of death.

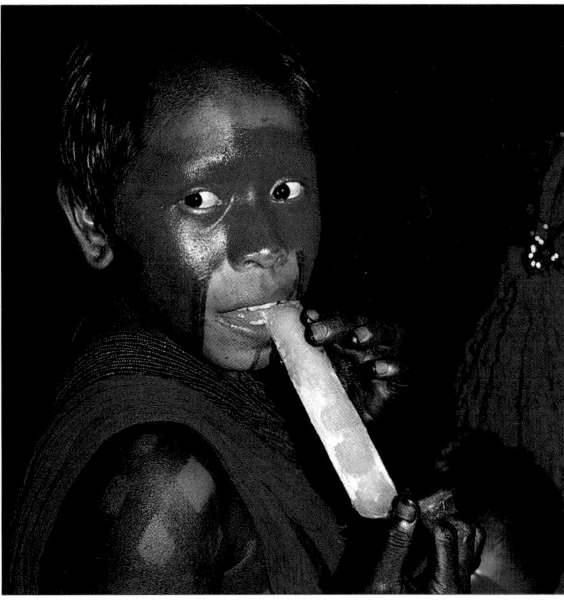

This Kayapo child from the rain forests of Brazil, in South America, is wearing face paint made from plants.

Plants in the bathroom

We use many plants in our bathrooms. Soaps, shampoos, moisturising creams and make-up all contain plant oils. These plants include soya beans, sunflowers, coconut palms and olives. Toothpastes are often flavoured with mint, fennel or cloves.

Sweet smells

One of the most valuable things about plants is their smell. Not all smell good, of course, but those that do have been used to scent clothes, rooms, hair and skin for thousands of years. Many perfumes come from the flowers of plants such as rose, jasmine and orange.

Plants that cure us

For most of our history, plants have cured many illnesses. In countries like Britain, we now use many man-made medicines. In other parts of the world, people still rely on medicines made from local plants.

The herbalist Nicholas Culpeper (1616-54)

Herbals

Centuries ago, before there were doctors and surgeons, some people used a wide range of plants as cures for illnesses. These people (known as herbalists) had a vast knowledge of the plants they used. They put their knowledge into books called herbals. One of the most famous herbals was written by Nicholas Culpeper and published in 1653.

The herbalists had some ideas that modern scientists find hard to accept. They believed, for example, that certain medicines only worked when the planets were in certain positions.

Different cures

Wych (pronounced 'witch') hazel has antiseptic qualities which make it good for cleaning wounds. It was used by the native North Americans to treat many complaints, from back-ache to ulcers. They used extracts from the bark and leaves to prevent swelling and stop bleeding.

The painkiller called aspirin was first made from the leaves and bark of the white willow. The ancient Greeks and native North Americans used it long ago. It has been used to treat pains like toothache, earache and headache. Modern aspirin is now made artificially with chemicals based on those found in the willow.

Oil extracted from the evening primrose is used as a remedy for arthritis, migraine, asthma, eczema and high blood pressure.

Wych hazel

Every part of henbane is poisonous and yet it has a long tradition of being used as a medicine. The plant contains chemicals used to relieve travel sickness and stomach pain. It has been used to treat some forms of mental illness.

Barefoot medicine

In countries like Britain, we still use some plant remedies, but most of our medicines are artificially made. In other parts of the world, people still use medicines from plants. In China, traditional (or 'barefoot') medicine is part of the country's health-care system. There are several special gardens where around 5000 medicinal plants are grown.

Traditional plant medicines on sale in China.

Evening primrose

Periwinkle was once used to treat inflammations of the skin.

Rain forest medicine chest

The indians of the rain forests have survived for thousands of years using a large number of medicinal plants found in their natural home. One group uses over a hundred different plants. The rain forests are rich in plants that may be useful to modern medicine, but only a few have been examined. Already the forests have given us remedies for malaria and drugs that have helped in the treatment of cancer, diabetes, Hodgkins's disease and snake bites. It is hoped that the rain forests may yet give us cures for other diseases.

Plants we use every day

Throughout our history we have used plants to make our homes, clothes, furniture, tools, games and musical instruments. Artificial materials are now common, but in some parts of the world people still use locally grown plants in their everyday lives.

Plants in the home

Inside our homes are hundreds of things made with plants. There are baskets made of thin willow stems; chairs made of rattan (the stems of a climbing plant from the rain forests); floor and wall tiles made from the bark of the cork oak; carpets made of cotton; paints and varnishes made with plant oils; doormats made of coconut fibres.

Plants for writing on

Another everyday material that comes from plants is paper. Today, most paper is made from wood which has had its bark removed. The wood is made into a pulp by machines or with chemicals. Bank notes, which need to be strong and long-lasting, are made from hemp, flax and cotton fibres.

Plant clothes

Clothes can be made from cotton plants. The cotton fibres are the fluffy white hairs on the seeds of the plant. The process of making fabrics from cotton has been carried out in India since 3000 BC. Linen is a material made from the stems of the flax plant.

Plants that shelter us

Wood is the plant material most commonly used to build homes. It is strong and flexible and lasts a long time. Where there is a good supply of timber, people make whole houses out of wood. In other places it is used for parts such as door frames, staircases and roof supports. Reeds, palms and bamboo are also used to make houses.

The Marsh Arabs of Iraq have built their houses out of reeds for centuries. In the foreground are reed mats ready to be sold.

Key

① *cane chair*
② *wicker basket*
③ *cotton cushion*
④ *wooden baseball bat*
⑤ *paper shade*
⑥ *paper pad*
⑦ *wooden frame*
⑧ *cotton curtain*

Plants at play

When we play sports and games, or paint pictures, we may well be using plants. Sports equipment is often made with artificial materials, but cricket bats are still made with wood from the willow tree. The best baseball bats are made of ash wood. Oil paints contain oils of linseed, poppyseed or sunflower seed. Musical instruments are made from a vast variety of woods; some wind instruments use reeds in their mouthpieces.

Bamboo everywhere

Every day, nearly half the world's population uses something made out of bamboo. It is used to make window frames, mats and screens, furniture, fans, paper, water pipes, storage vessels and musical instruments. It can also be eaten! Young bamboo shoots are used in Chinese cookery.

Keeping gardens

All over the world, throughout the centuries, people have had gardens. Often they have been used for growing useful plants, but most gardens are kept for pleasure. In Britain, gardening for pleasure first became popular in the sixteenth century.

Trade in plants

The first ornamental gardens kept only local plants. As transport improved, so people began to trade in plants. Gardeners in Europe in the sixteenth century were fascinated by plants from Asia and America. A botanist went on every new trip. Eventually, plant sellers were sending collectors abroad to find new plants.

A harmful trade

Today, as in the past, many plants are taken from one country to be sold in another. Sadly, sometimes too many plants are removed. They become rare in the wild. In Britain, there are laws against picking wild flowers and plants. We should only buy plants grown in garden nurseries. However, there are many reasons why plants become extinct. Some plants have been saved from extinction because they were grown in gardens.

This orchid from Costa Rica, in Central America, is endangered due to the trade in wild plants.

Gardens for all

All over the world, there are public gardens and parks for people to enjoy. Most people like to have plants near them and enjoy looking after them. People can grow plants wherever they are. If they have no garden, they use window boxes or pots on windowsills.

In this garden in Paris, France, someone has made the most of a little space above some windows.

Looking after the soil

To stay healthy, plants need certain minerals from the soil (see page 8). Healthy soil also has creatures such as worms which help plants to grow. Gardeners look after the soil by putting back the nutrients that the plants use up. This can be done by adding artificial fertilizers, but some people prefer to use natural compost or animal manure. Compost is made up of rotting plant material and kitchen waste, such as carrot tops and tea leaves.

Compost or manure need to be dug into the soil, at least once a year, to keep it healthy.

Gardener's ideas

Gardeners are always looking for ways of growing more successful plants and for destroying diseases and pests. Many believe that seeds should be planted before the new moon. The growing moon, as it goes from new to full, is thought to help the plants to grow. Gardeners also believe in 'green fingers'. A person with 'green fingers' is said to be particularly good at making things grow.

Words to remember

Botanist – a person who studies plants where they grow.

Plants and fossils

Fossils are the remains of plants and animals that lived millions of years ago. The plant fossils that we have found show us roughly how plants have developed over time.

Many plants of the past no longer exist. Others live today, but look very different to how they once were. This is because they have adapted over the years to changing conditions. A few have hardly changed at all.

Changing through time

Among the earliest plant fossils are those of blue-green algae. They lived in the Earth's waters about 3000 million years ago. These plants began to make oxygen and it was this gas that later made animal life on Earth possible.

Plants began to live on land about 400 million years ago. Gradually, they developed stiffer, woody stems which enabled them to reach towards the light. These early plants were quite small, forming forests only one metre high.

Larger plants covered the land about 345–280 million years ago. Ferns, horsetails and lycopods grew to the size of very large trees. Then came the conifers. Flowering plants appeared 140 million years ago. By 65 million years ago the world's forests looked much the same as they do now.

Extinction

Flowering plants are now the most successful group of plants. Many plants have become extinct. Some members of the earlier groups of plants still survive, but they often look different. For example, we still have ferns, horsetails and lycopods today, but they are much smaller plants than the great trees they once were.

About 300 million years ago, large parts of the Earth were covered with forests of large ferns, lycopods and horsetails. Their fossils form the black 'rock' which we burn: coal.

Living fossils

Some of these surviving plants have not changed very much over time. They are called living fossils. Ginkgos must have been eaten by plant-eating dinosaurs and they look much the same today.

Many of the modern plants we have today developed between 136 and 65 million years ago. Fossils of these plants can tell us a lot about how the climate has changed since then. For example, we may find a fossil of a plant that today likes damp, hot conditions. The fossil may be found in a desert area. This suggests that, a long time ago, the desert was the site of a tropical rain forest.

Ginkgos are only found in the wild in one tiny area of China, but they are grown in parks and gardens all over the world.

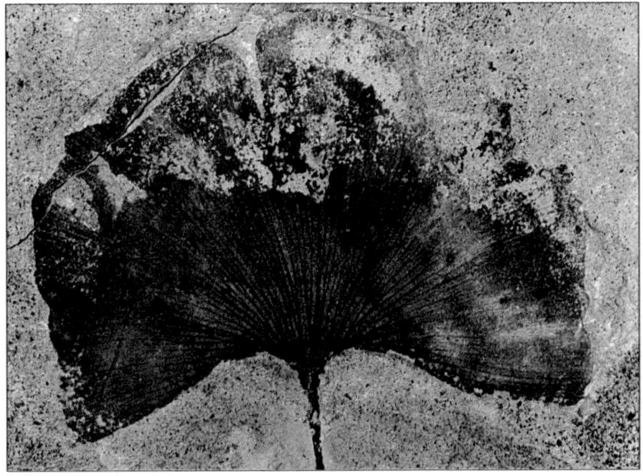

This fossil ginkgo leaf shows that the plant has changed little over time.

Saving our plants

We owe our lives to plants; we could not survive without them. Yet we don't always treat them very well. Thousands of plants are in danger of extinction. This is usually because their habitats are being harmed or destroyed. It makes more sense to look after plants.

The Earth needs plants

Plants make their own food. They are the most successful and largest group of living things that can do this. Plants are the first link in most food chains; without them there would be no food. Plants also make oxygen in the air. We need this gas to breath.

Plants' roots hold the soil together and stop it being washed away by torrential rain. The leaves that fall from the plants enrich the soil.

Plants are often the first living things to move on to lands that have been damaged. This damage can happen naturally, by the eruption of a volcano, for example, or by the actions of human beings.

Losing plants

Every year, more natural habitats are removed. They are cleared to make room for houses, roads, factories, fields and shops. We also spoil what it left by polluting the soil, the water and the air. As a result, we lose plants and animals.

In some parts of the world, people are trying to stop the destruction and mend the damage. They are cutting down on pollution, putting plants back into their proper environment or simply leaving areas alone so that plants can grow back on their own. They are also trying to preserve what has not been harmed in reserves and national parks. Worldwide, there are many thousands of natural habitats that are now protected by law.

What can we do?

We can all do something to save plants. For example, we can try to be less wasteful by buying less and recycling more. In particular, we can try to waste less paper. We can try not to buy products made from plants that are rare. We can act locally to protect patches of wild land from harm, and we can grow our own plants. The smallest garden can give many plants and animals the chance to live. If you do not have a garden, use a pot on a windowsill (see page 43). Growing just one seed, and tending to the plant that grows from it, is a valuable thing to do.

All over the world, people are planting trees in an effort to give our planet a green future.

◀ *Plants are lost when the habitat in which they live is destroyed. They are also killed by pollution. In this river in Tasmania, the plants have been killed by copper pollution.*

Published by BBC Educational Publishing, a division of BBC Education, BBC White City, 201 Wood Lane, London W12 7TS

First published in this form 1997

Colour reproduction by Dot Gradations, UK

Acknowledgements
Edited by Debbie Reid
Designed by Charlotte Crace
Picture research by Helen Taylor

Illustrations: © Martine Collings 1995 (pages 6, 7, 12, 13, 19, 26 and 30-1) © Charles Raymond 1995 (pages 4-5, 10, 15, 21, 24, 25, 28, 33, 34-5, 38, 39, 40-1 and 44-5); © John Shipperbottom 1995 (page 22)

Photos: A-Z Botanical Collection Ltd **pp. 2 (bottom), 9, (bottom), 25;** Ardea London **pp. 18, 32 (left);** Bruce Colman Ltd **pp. 12, 23, 45 (top);** Ecoscene **p. 47;** Mary Evans Picture Library **p. 38;** Luke Finn **pp. 17, 36, 37 (top);** Garden Picture Library **pp. 42, 43 (top);** Garden/Wildlife Matters Photographic Library **pp. 20, 43 (bottom);** Robert Harding Picture Library **pp. 8, 41;** Hutchinson Library **p. 39;** Natural History Museum **p. 43 (bottom);** NHPA **pp. 3, 9 (top), 16 (top), 29 (bottom), 31, 32 (right), 33, 35, 46;** Planet Earth Pictures **pp. 2 (top), 11, 14, 16 (bottom), 24, 27, 29 (top), 37 (bottom)**

ANIMALS

Written by
Robin Robbins

Illustrated by
John Dunne, Martin Knowelden,
Sean Milne and Sally Olding

CONTENTS

The animal kingdom

Scientists have divided the animal kingdom into large groups called classes. Each class is made up of different animal species which are alike in important ways. This book introduces you to most of the classes, and helps you to understand how the animal kingdom is divided.

What is an animal?

Not all animals have fur. Many have bare skin, shells, feathers or their skeletons outside their bodies. Some have babies which grow inside them, while others lay eggs to make more animals of the same kind.

The animals on these pages are very different from each other, but there is one thing they all have in common. They eat their food by taking it inside their bodies. This is the simplest way to tell whether a living thing is really an animal or not.

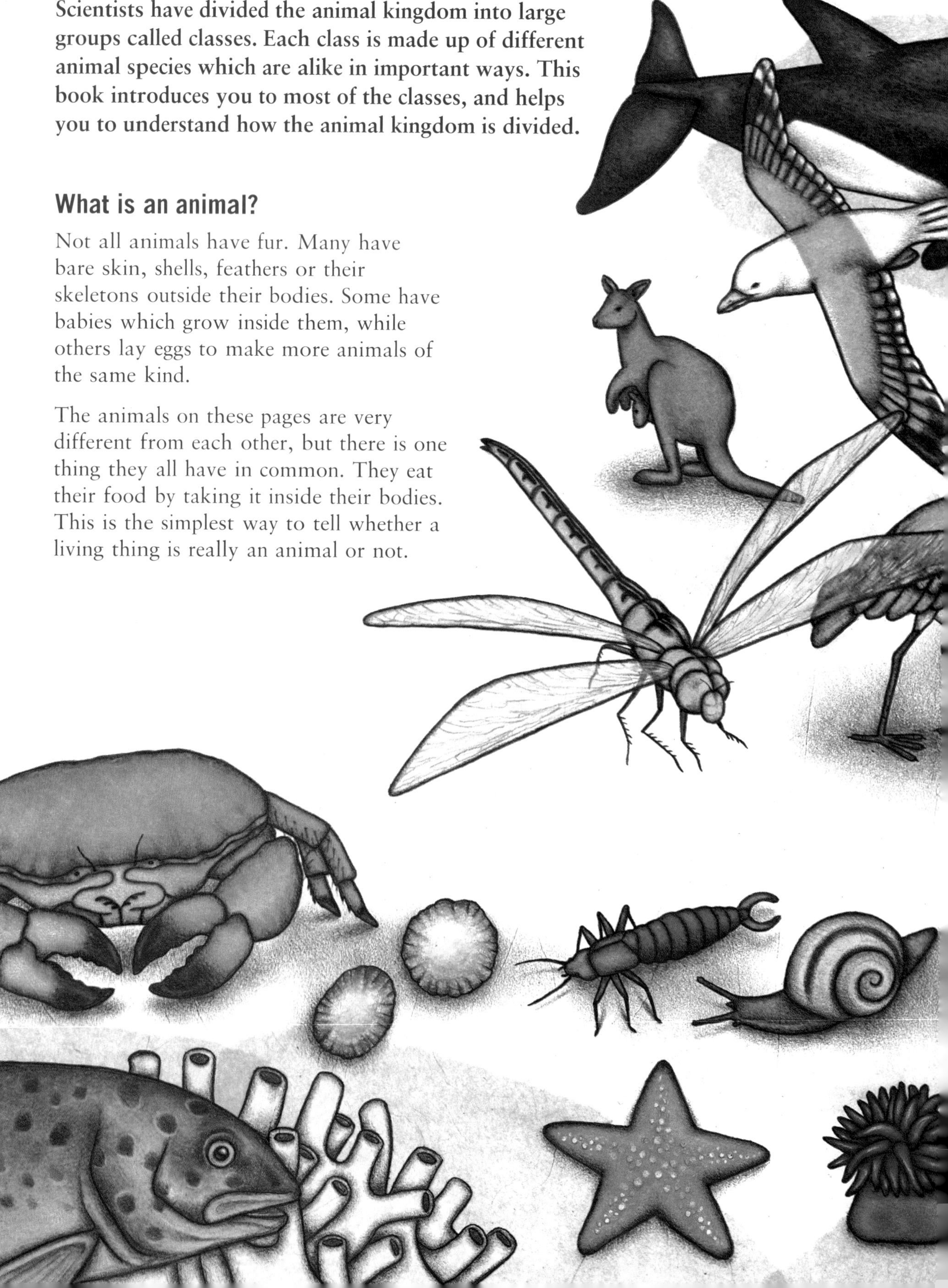

Worms

Worms may not seem the most exciting of animals. You may even think they all look rather similar! But there are three quite separate worm classes, which live very different lives.

Annelid worms

Annelids are worms whose bodies are divided up into rings called segments. They live in the sea, in ponds and on land. The kind we see most often are the earthworms that live in the soil.

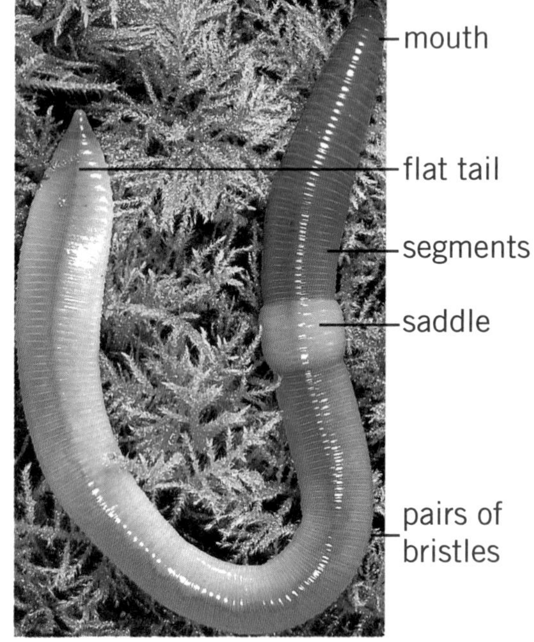

Earthworm

Earthworms are very much alike, so you must look closely to spot small differences in shape and colour. They all have flat tails and a mouth underneath at the pointed end. Adult earthworms also have a 'saddle' where eggs are made.

If you run a finger along the underside of a worm, you can feel lots of pairs of bristles. These are used to grip the ground as the worm moves along. Amazingly the worm moves by pushing the liquid inside its body from the back end to the front and back again. This causes its body to stretch forward and then bunch up as it crawls along. The bristles grip the ground at one end while the other end changes shape.

You sometimes see gulls marching on the spot on wet fields or sand. Worms sense the movement, which probably feels like rain, and up they wriggle to become food for the gull! On a damp day, try trampling for worms yourself. Test to find the most successful worm-charming place.

Earthworms are very important to gardeners and farmers. Their burrows let air and water into the soil, and they pull dead leaves down into the ground to eat. This helps to keep the soil mixed, while the worms' body waste adds to the goodness of the soil.

Many birds hunt for worms in the grass.

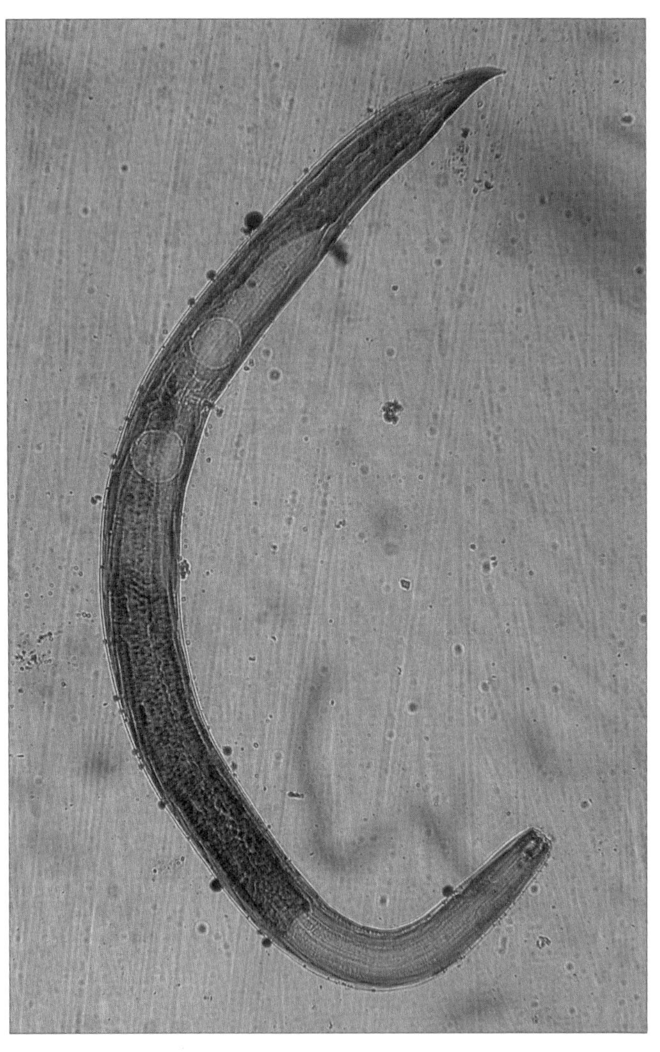

Nematode worms

You will need a microscope to see most of these tiny worms. Nematodes are not related to earthworms and their bodies are not divided up into segments. There are probably more nematodes in the world than any other animal, with about 90 000 in one rotten apple and millions in every square metre of soil. Some nematodes are parasites, living and getting their food from inside another living thing. Indeed most plants and animals have nematodes living inside them.

Tiny nematodes can be found among rotting plants.

Flatworms

Flatworms live only in damp or watery places. Their bodies do not have segments, and they either eat other small creatures or live as parasites inside bigger animals. If you go pond dipping, you are sure to see flatworms oozing along in your catch tray.

There are several different kinds of flatworms.

Millipedes and centipedes

You will have to look carefully to spot the main difference between a millipede and a centipede. They both have bodies divided up into segments and lots of legs. But if you look closely at a millipede, you will see that it has two pairs of legs to each segment. The centipede has only one pair.

Millipedes and centipedes prefer to live in damp places, so look for them under rotting wood or big stones. Those found in this kind of habitat will have rather flat bodies, with legs spread out on either side. Other kinds live in holes in the ground. Can you guess what shape their bodies and legs might be?

The millipede's legs move in a wave.

When collecting millipedes and centipedes to study, put each one in a separate jar with some wet moss, because they will die if they dry out. You must remember to return them to their habitats as soon as you have finished looking at them.

Centipedes can move much more quickly than millipedes.

Use a magnifying lens to compare heads. The millipede has short antennae, which bend down to touch and feel the ground as it walks. Not all millipedes have eyes, and even those that do cannot see particularly well.

The centipede has longer antennae. It uses them to feel things as it hunts for small creatures to eat. To stun its prey, the centipede uses the poisonous pincers that curve round its head.

British centipedes are too small to hurt people, but in tropical countries there are some very big species which can give humans a painful bite.

All millipedes are plant-eating animals, so not even the big tropical ones will bite you. But for protection, many millipedes release nasty-tasting chemicals when they are touched. This does not always work, and birds and other animals may still eat them.

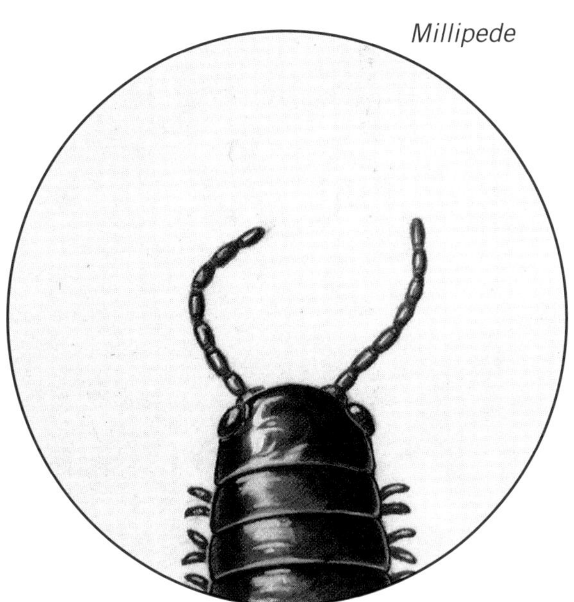

Millipede

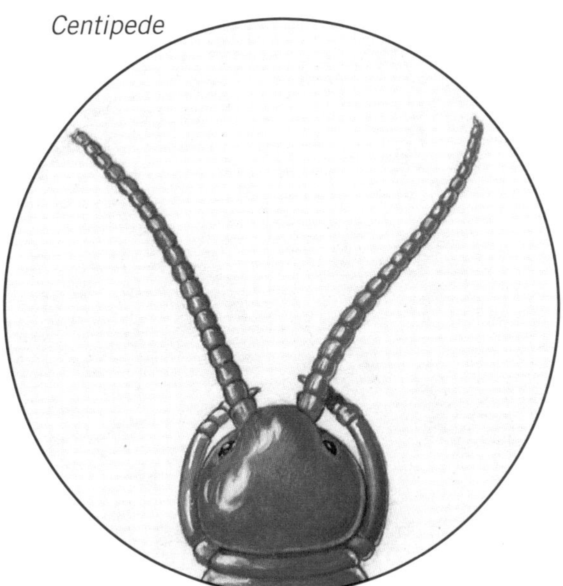

Centipede

Mind-boggler

Did you know that centipedes can make good mothers? Some kinds lay their eggs in tiny underground 'caves'. They wrap themselves round the eggs and then lick them to keep them clean.

This centipede is protecting her eggs in an underground 'cave'.

What is an insect?

There are more insects in the world than all the other animals put together. Scientists already know more than a million species, and new ones are being discovered every day. But the lives of common insects still hold secrets that anyone can explore in a park or a garden.

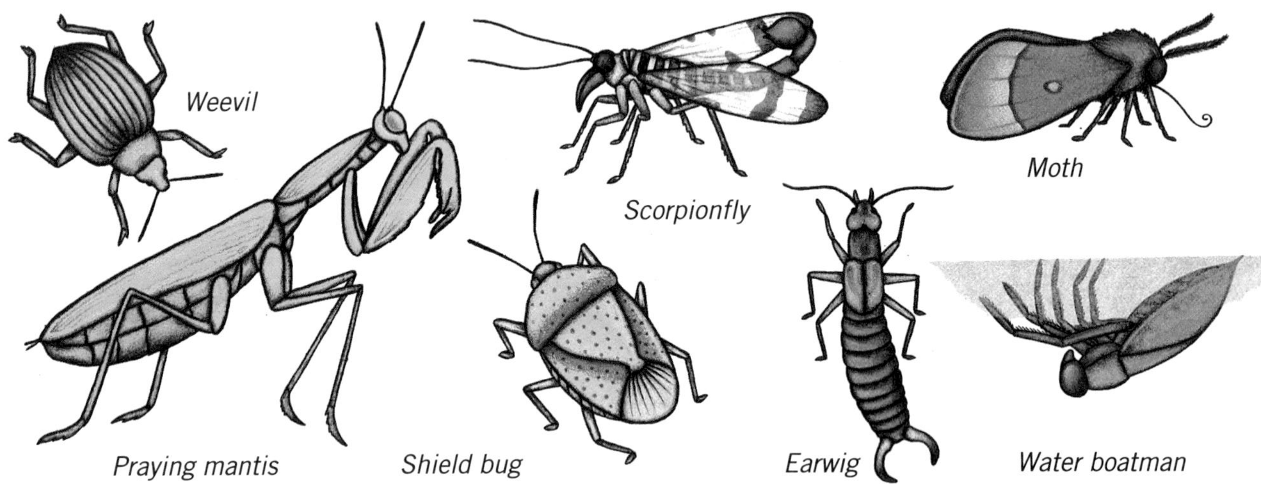

The class of insects includes some of the most beautiful and interesting animals that you can imagine. Each insect is built to the same basic plan. Their bodies are divided into three parts: the head, thorax and abdomen. All adults have six jointed legs, while some of the young do not have legs at all. Insects have no skeleton inside, but they do have a hard outer skin called an exoskeleton. Almost all insects have one or two pairs of wings, although not all of them bother to fly!

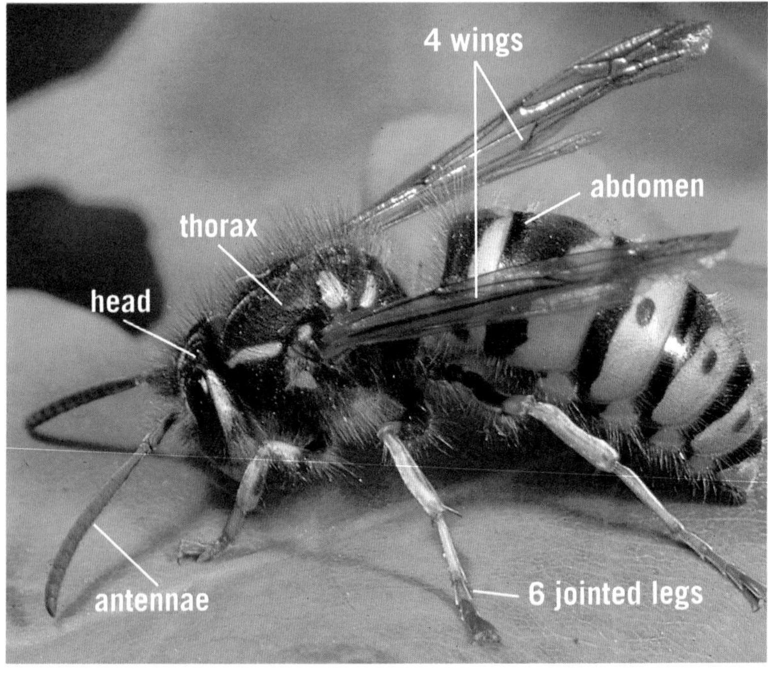

Common wasp

Looking closer

If you find a dead insect, a magnifying lens will help you to discover how it once lived. For clues about the food it ate, look at the mouthparts.

Butterflies and moths have a spiral 'drinking straw' called a proboscis to drink nectar from flowers.

Bugs spike plants and other animals with their sharp beaks and suck out their juices.

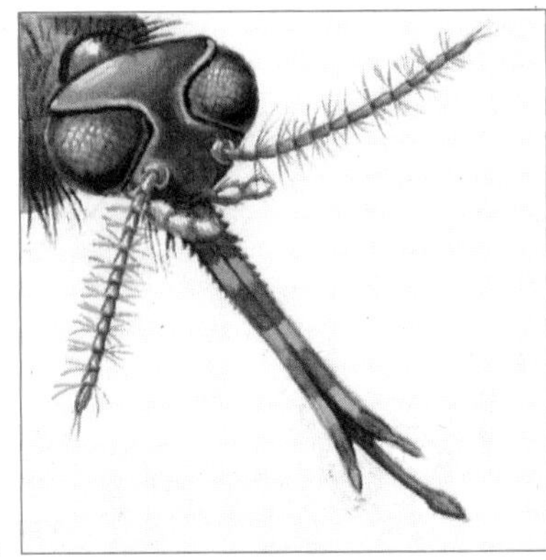

Flies spit on their food to dissolve it, then lap it up with their flat stubby tongues.

Now look at the insect's two large eyes. These are made up of hundreds of tiny eyes, each seeing a slightly different picture all round the insect's head. The result is rather blurry, but just try to creep up on a dragonfly if you want to see how well it works!

Between the two large eyes you will find three smaller ones. Although these do not work very well, they can tell light from darkness.

Can you see this dragonfly's eyes?

Metamorphosis

Young insects do not usually look at all like their parents. They may even eat different foods and live in different habitats. A great change must take place before they become adults. This change is called metamorphosis.

Insects such as ladybirds have four stages to their metamorphosis. The young insects are called larvae.

① The female ladybird lays her yellow eggs in little groups under a leaf.

② About a week later, the larvae climb from the eggs and begin to eat the aphids. As each larva feeds and grows, its skin becomes too tight and splits. There is a new skin underneath.

③ The skin splits for the last time, and underneath is the pupa. Although it looks very still, a wonderful change is taking place inside. The body turns almost completely to liquid and a new ladybird is made.

④ When the ladybird bursts out of the pupa, it is yellow and has no spots. But it will soon look just like its parents, and its metamorphosis will be complete.

The metamorphosis of a ladybird

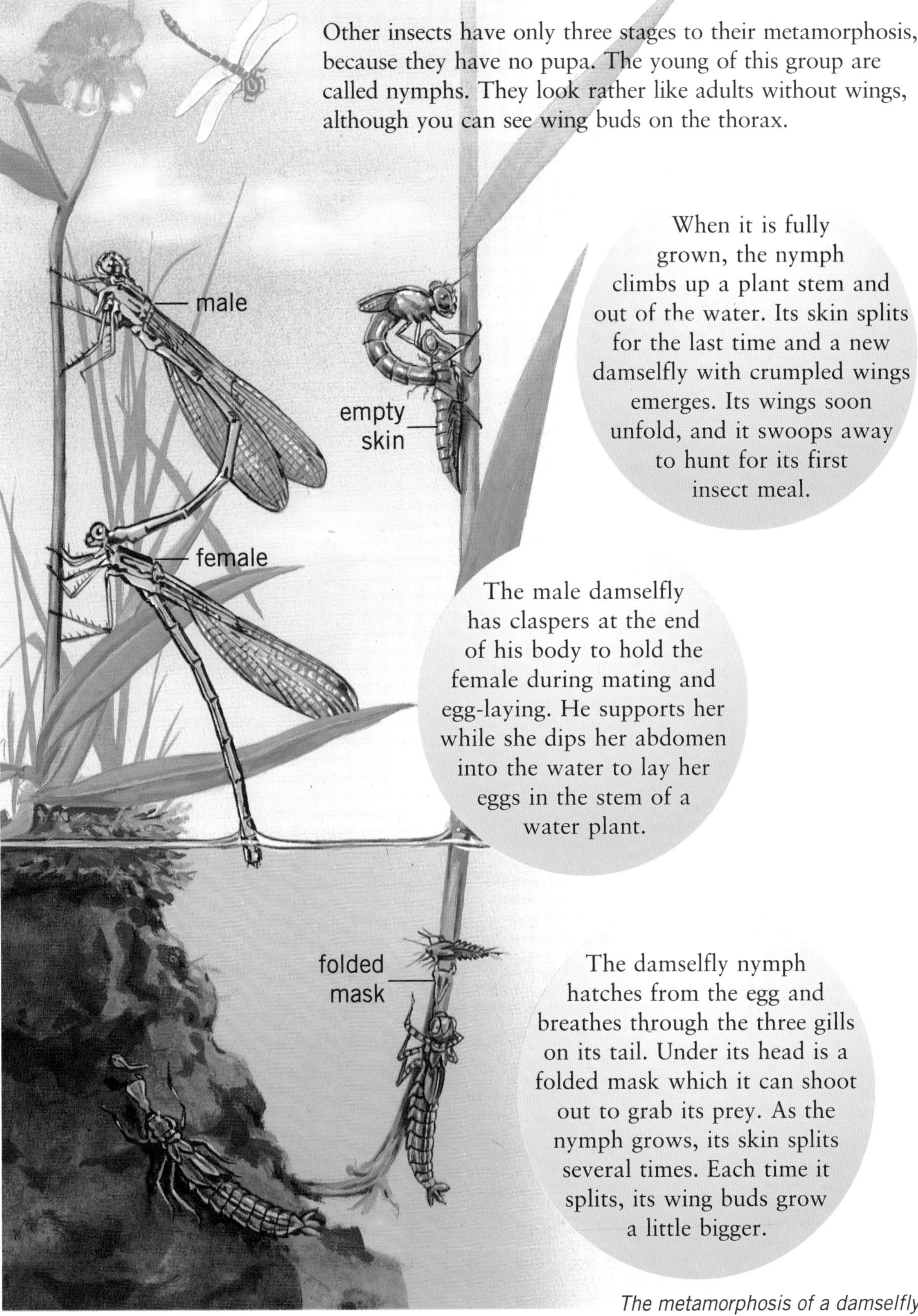

Other insects have only three stages to their metamorphosis, because they have no pupa. The young of this group are called nymphs. They look rather like adults without wings, although you can see wing buds on the thorax.

When it is fully grown, the nymph climbs up a plant stem and out of the water. Its skin splits for the last time and a new damselfly with crumpled wings emerges. Its wings soon unfold, and it swoops away to hunt for its first insect meal.

The male damselfly has claspers at the end of his body to hold the female during mating and egg-laying. He supports her while she dips her abdomen into the water to lay her eggs in the stem of a water plant.

The damselfly nymph hatches from the egg and breathes through the three gills on its tail. Under its head is a folded mask which it can shoot out to grab its prey. As the nymph grows, its skin splits several times. Each time it splits, its wing buds grow a little bigger.

The metamorphosis of a damselfly

How insects live

Some insects live together and share the work of running the community. They include ants, termites and some kinds of bees and wasps. We call these 'social insects'.

Living together

There are three kinds of ant in the black ants' nest.

Worker ants just work all day! These female ants nurse the young and dig new tunnels. They soon die, but there are always new worker ants to replace them.

Male ants do not work. On a hot summer day they and the new queens swarm out and take a mating flight. Once they have mated, the males die.

When the queen has mated, she scrapes her wings off against something hard and finds a place for a new nest. She then rests until the Spring, when she will lay her eggs and nurse the first young ants. The new worker ants will grow up to take over all the duties of the nest, while the queen spends the rest of her life just laying eggs.

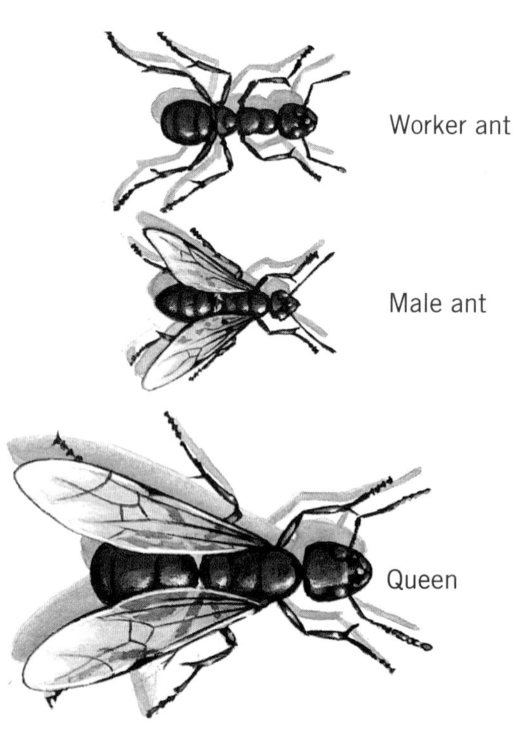

These worker ants are looking after the larvae. Close by is an unmated queen.

Keeping Safe

Many animals enjoy eating juicy insects. But insects have wonderful ways to keep themselves safe.

They surprise

The click beetle pretends to be dead, then suddenly clicks into a somersault, shocking its predator into dropping it.

The click beetle can be found in most hedgerows.

They hide

The grasshopper's green-and-brown colour means it can hide in the grass. Even if its chirp gives it away, the grasshopper can use its long back legs to spring out of reach.

Butterflies hide by folding their wings to the camouflaged undersides. To attract a mate, they simply open them out and display their beautiful colours.

The grasshopper is camouflaged in the grass.

Adult hover-flies feed from flowers.

They hurt

Some insects bite or sting, while others are prickly to eat. Although one insect may die when a young predator first tries to eat it, its death will protect other insects of the same kind.

They cheat

Animals know that wasps can sting. This harmless hover-fly has yellow-and-black stripes so that birds will leave it alone.

They warn

Ladybirds taste horrible! Their bright colours remind predators of an earlier, unpleasant meal.

In spite of this, millions of insects are eaten every day. But, of course, millions of eggs are laid by their parents to replace them.

Arachnids

Spiders, harvestmen, scorpions, ticks, mites and horseshoe crabs all belong to the class of arachnids. Arachnids are predators with biting fangs, an exoskeleton and eight legs. In most cases, their bodies are in two parts. They have a head and thorax joined into one and an abdomen.

Spiders

There are over six hundred different species of spider in Britain. Although they all spin silk, not all of them make webs to catch their food.

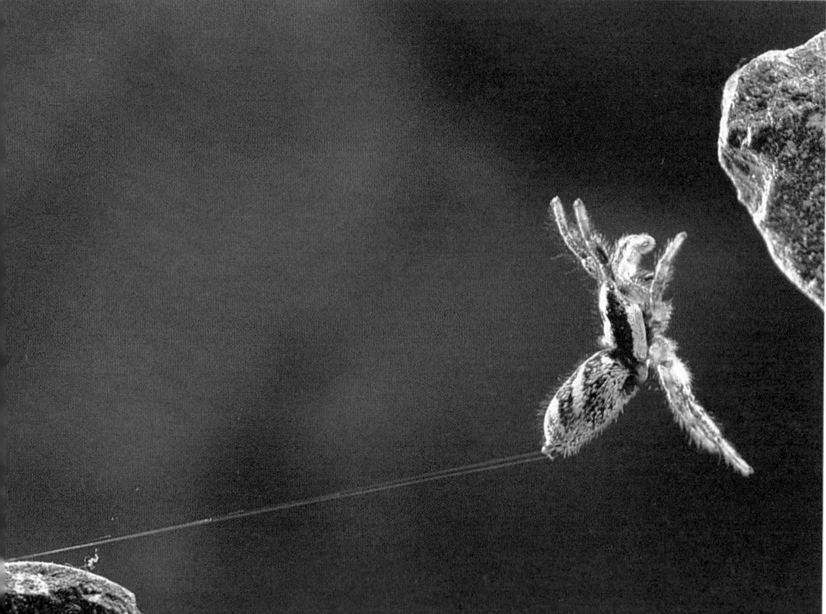

The little zebra spider hunts for food on a warm sunny wall or rockery. It uses its silk to make a safety line to stop itself from falling. The zebra spider stalks small insects, ending the hunt by jumping suddenly on its prey. Very good eyesight is needed for this, so the spider has eight eyes, including two extra-big ones at the front.

The black-and-white zebra spider belongs to a group known as jumping spiders.

Harvestmen

Harvestmen may look like spiders but they are not closely related and cannot spin silk. Their bodies have only one part and their eyes are perched on top. The harvestman traps its prey with its legs. It crushes it down and then bites off small pieces with a pair of pincers at the front of its body.

Look out for harvestmen in long grass and around stones.

Other arachnids

It is easy to find tiny water mites swimming along in the pond. Water mites are carnivorous animals and hunt for other small creatures to eat. They pierce them with their fangs before sucking out the insides.

There are over two hundred different kinds of water mites in Britain. They are very small, but a magnifier will show you how beautifully patterned they are.

Most water mites are brightly coloured.

The pseudoscorpion eats land-living mites which it finds among rotting leaves. It looks like a miniature version of the scorpion found in hot countries, but it has no stinging tail.

The pseudoscorpion is less than 5 mm long.

Spot the difference

Make careful sketches of spiders' webs found on grass, bushes, buildings and walls. Each type of spider spins its own special web. With practice, you can decide who made the web without even seeing the spider!

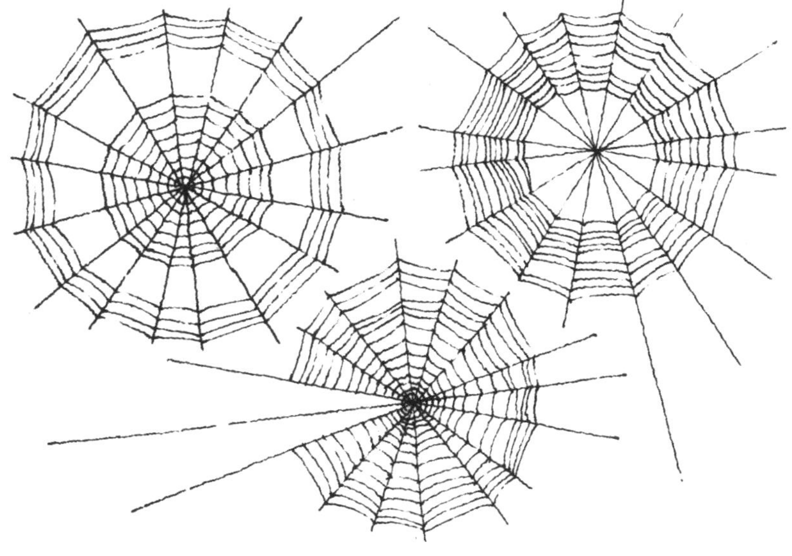

Many webs have sticky strands to trap the spider's prey.

Crustaceans

Crustaceans have hard outer shells, which are usually jointed so the animals can move easily. It isn't always possible to see that their bodies are divided into three parts. They have two pairs of feelers, and in most cases ten legs. The front legs of lobsters and crabs have evolved into pincers. Almost all crustaceans live in water.

American lobster

Woodlice

Woodlice are perhaps the easiest crustaceans to study. You can find them under any damp stone in a park or garden. They will often be huddled up together or pushed into cracks in logs or between stones. They do this to stop too much air from getting around their bodies, because they will die if they get too dry.

Crustacean shells are not stretchy, so a crustacean must shed its old tight shell as it grows bigger. Underneath is a new, larger shell. Sometimes you find a woodlouse that is half white and half grey. It has already shed one half of its shell, and the other white piece will soon drop off.

This woodlouse is shedding its old white shell.

Like many water-living crustaceans, such as the prawn in the picture below, female woodlice carry their eggs and pale young under their bodies.

Barnacles cement themselves to the rocks and never travel again.

Mind-boggler

Seaside barnacles are crustaceans which are hanging upside-down! As larvae they swim in the sea, but later they fasten themselves onto the rocks, where they stay for the rest of their lives. Their plated shells are the part you see when the tide is out. But once underwater, their legs come out from between the plates and wave about to collect their microscopic food.

Molluscs

Molluscs are animals with soft bodies. They include slugs, snails, mussels, whelks and squids. Molluscs have a head, a strong foot and a mantle. The mantle is a kind of soft bag that covers all or part of the body.

Some molluscs are only as big as a pinhead, while the biggest ones are more than 5 metres long! Most have a shell, although often this is hidden inside or is very small. Bivalve molluscs live in water and have two shells hinged together.

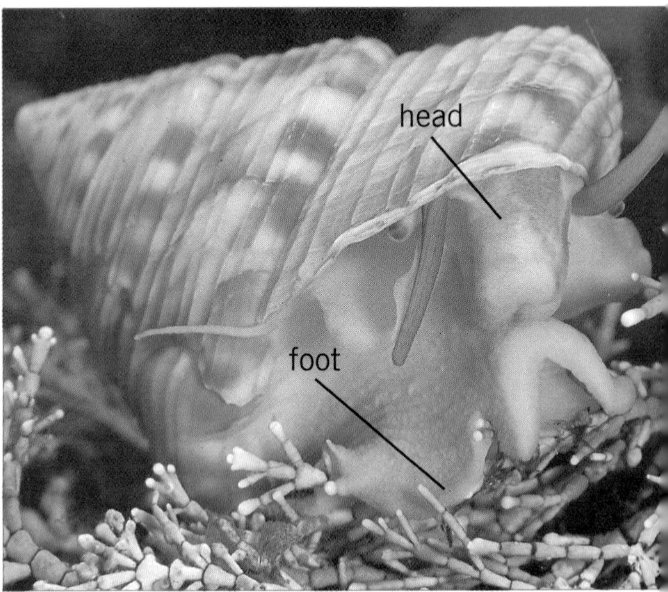

Painted topshells live in the sea.

In the garden

Because slugs do not have a shell, either inside or out, they have no way to protect themselves from drying out and must always stay in damp places.

You can collect different slug species with a soft paintbrush. Put the slugs in a container with wet leaves while you study them with a magnifying lens. Their skins have beautiful colours and patterns, and you may enjoy painting a slug portrait gallery!

Slugs can be sorted into two main groups. Keeled slugs are ridged along the back, like the bottom of a boat, while round-backed slugs have no ridge. Both these groups feed on plants.

You might be lucky enough to find one of a third group, the carnivorous slugs. Their narrow heads let them follow earthworms into their burrows, where they eat them. Carnivorous slugs have tiny shells at the tips of their tails.

Keeled slug

Round-backed slug

Carnivorous slug

On the beach

In rock pools, winkles and limpets graze a trail through the seaweeds on the rocks. When the tide goes out, each limpet returns to the safety of a made-to-measure dent, which it scrapes in the rock with the help of its shell.

Carnivorous whelks eat other marine molluscs by boring holes through their shells. They particularly like bivalve molluscs, such as the tellins which live just below the surface of the sand.

These carnivorous dog whelks eat dead sea animals as well as molluscs.

Mind-boggler

The octopus is a mollusc too! Its strong foot has evolved into a set of eight tentacles, which it uses to catch its prey. The octopus has no shell, but it can see well and has a good brain.

The octopus has suckers on its tentacles. These help it to cling tightly to the rocks.

Fish

There are fish in the seas, rivers and ponds all over the world. Although we speak of 'fish' as if they are all closely related, there are three quite different groups.

Jawless fish, such as the lamprey, have toothed suckers instead of jaws. They use the suckers to fasten themselves onto other fish to feed.

This lamprey has fastened itself onto a shark and is sucking out its blood.

Fish with skeletons of cartilage, which is softer than bone, include the sharks, rays, dogfish and skates. They have no flaps over their gills, and their scales have rough edges like teeth. Their tail fins are not symmetrical.

Smooth scales help the roach to swim easily through the water.

Fish with bony skeletons make up the largest group, with more than twenty thousand different kinds. Most have smooth scales and flaps over their gills. Their tails are symmetrical.

The fish in your tank

Aquarium fish soon learn to come to one corner of the tank every day if you always feed them in that spot. Choose the nearest corner so you can observe and sketch their adaptations to a watery life.

Watch a fish taking water into its mouth and gulping hard. This squeezes the water over the gills and out through the gill covers. As the water goes through the fish's body, oxygen is taken into the blood.

How a fish breathes

Compare the body of a fish to that of a submarine. This special streamlined shape allows for easy movement in the water. See how the scales overlap each other smoothly from front to back. This helps to reduce friction.

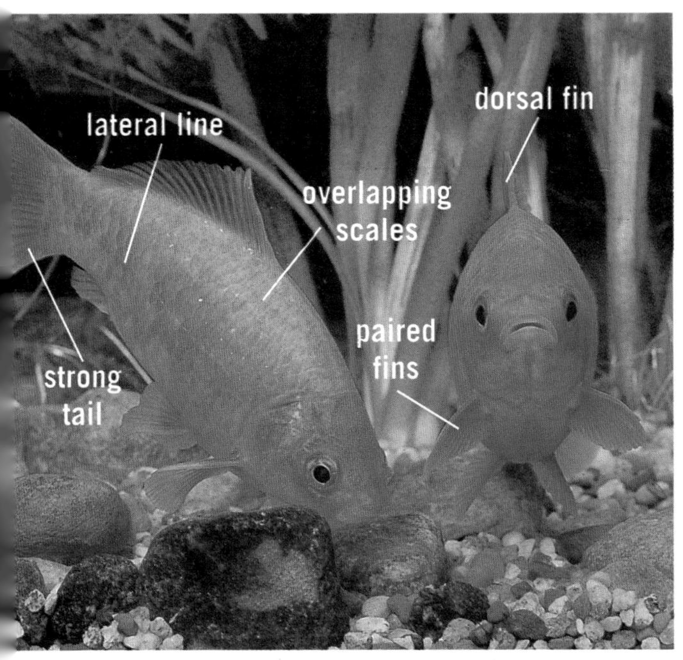

Watch the powerful tail acting as a propeller, while the fish's body flexes from side to side to help it along.

Check how the fish steers itself by moving its paired fins one at a time, like oars. Note that the dorsal fin flattens out as the fish speeds up, and is held high to keep it balanced when the fish is still.

Find the lateral line. This picks up vibrations to tell the fish that something is moving in the water nearby.

Goldfish search for food at the bottom of garden ponds.

Strange fish

Not all fish have the same streamlined shape. They may swim upright or lie flat on their sides, and there are even some kinds which can come out of the water!

Sea horse

The sea horse breaks all the rules. It swims upright, so it isn't streamlined like other fish, and its dorsal fin, not its tail, moves it along.

The sea horse is a camouflage magician and can change colour in seconds. It can also grow whispy pieces of skin when it needs them to help it hide in the seaweed.

Last but not least, female sea horses lay their eggs in a pouch in the male's body. It is he who looks after the eggs, until the babies are ready to come out.

Sea horses live mainly in tropical countries, but their relatives, the pipefish, are found around the coasts of Britain.

The sea horse keeps in one place by curling its tail round weeds and rocks.

European eel

The European eel can wriggle over the dewy Autumn grass to find a river to take it to the sea. It swims down the river and moves into salt water as it enters the Atlantic Ocean. The eel's journey finally takes it to the Sargasso Sea, where it breeds and then dies. Its eggs hatch and the young drift back across the ocean to grow up in the ponds and rivers of Europe. When they are old enough, they too will make this long, last journey.

The European eel is a fish out of water!

Deep-sea angler fish

This deep-sea angler fish lives in almost total darkness. But on its head it grows a 'fishing line', complete with a glowing light. Smaller fish are attracted to the light and are quickly gobbled up.

Deep-sea angler fish live only in the deepest oceans.

Plaice

The plaice, like other flatfish, starts life the same shape as ordinary fish. But it isn't long before one eye moves to the other side of its head, so that it has two eyes on the same side. The plaice then spends most of its time lying on the bottom of the sea with both eyes looking upward, and with its fins looking rather like a fringe round its body. The upper side of the fish changes colour to match the sand and gravel on which it lies. When it swims from one place to another, it takes only a couple of minutes to match its new resting place.

Flatfish, such as the plaice, live close to the bottom of the sea.

Amphibians

Amphibian is a word that means 'on both sides of life'. The name was given because most amphibians start their lives as eggs in water, and then hatch into tadpoles with gills for breathing. But when they are adult, amphibians can come out of the water and onto the land, where they breathe air through their lungs. They can also blot up oxygen through their damp bare skins. By doing this, some amphibians can stay underwater for a long time.

There are three groups of amphibians in the world: frogs and toads; newts and salamanders; and caecilians.

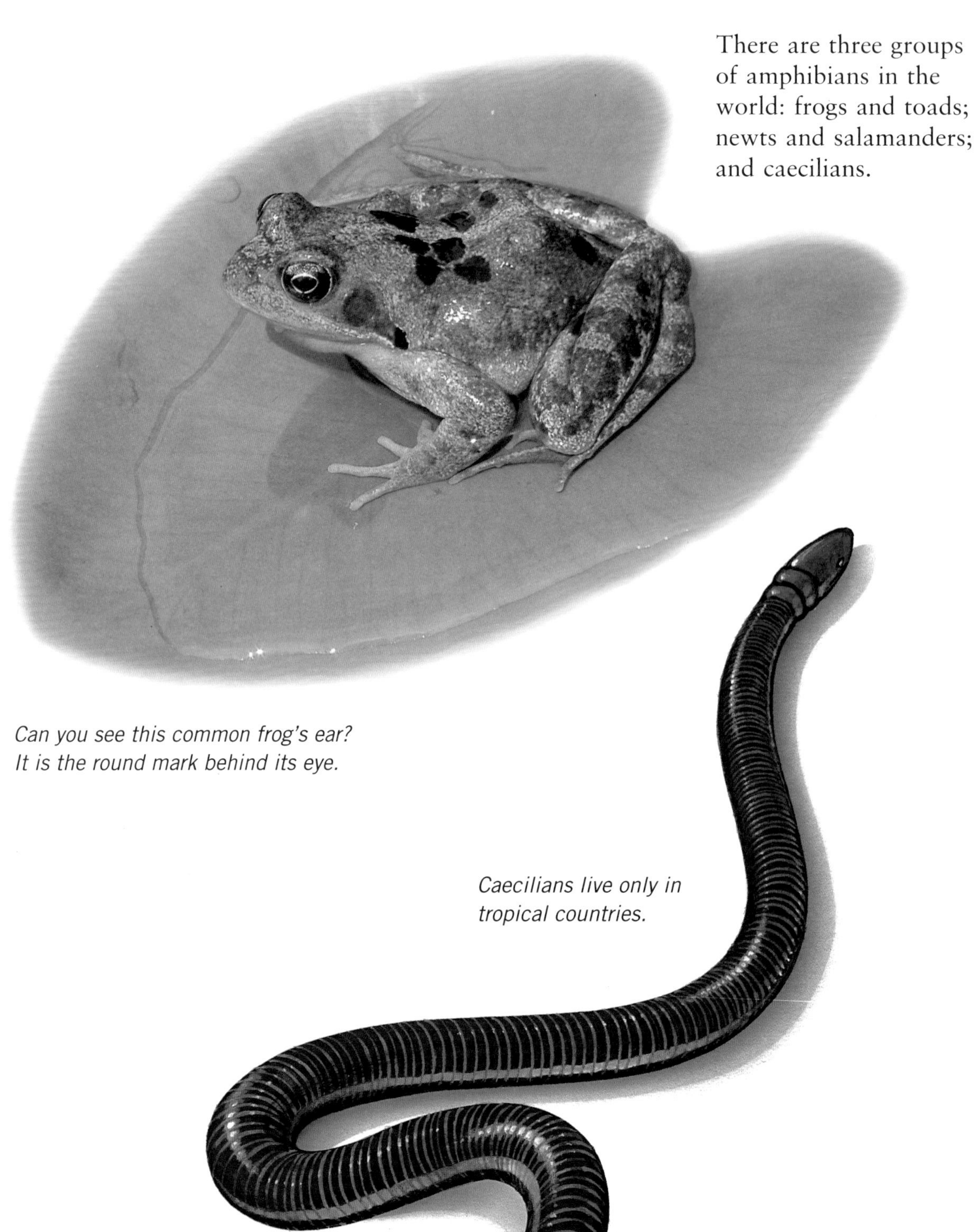

Can you see this common frog's ear? It is the round mark behind its eye.

Caecilians live only in tropical countries.

The common frog

In March you might go to a pond at dusk and hear male common frogs splashing about and calling to the females. At this time of year the male has a special rough pad on each hand to help him hold his slippery mate while she lays her spawn and he fertilizes it.

Frogspawn is laid in shallow water. At first it looks like a clump of black dots, which sink to the bottom of the pond. Soon the jelly protecting each dot swells in the water and the spawn floats up to the surface.

About a week later, the dots change shape and turn into tadpoles. The tadpoles have a frill of gills on both sides of their heads. A flap of skin will later grow over these and hide them, and the tadpoles will begin to eat other small creatures, dead or alive.

The froglet's back legs grow slowly, finally bending outwards like those of an adult frog. Its front legs grow inside the body and pop out from the gill covers when they are ready. About twelve weeks from the time the spawn was laid, the tail disappears and the tadpole's metamorphosis is complete.

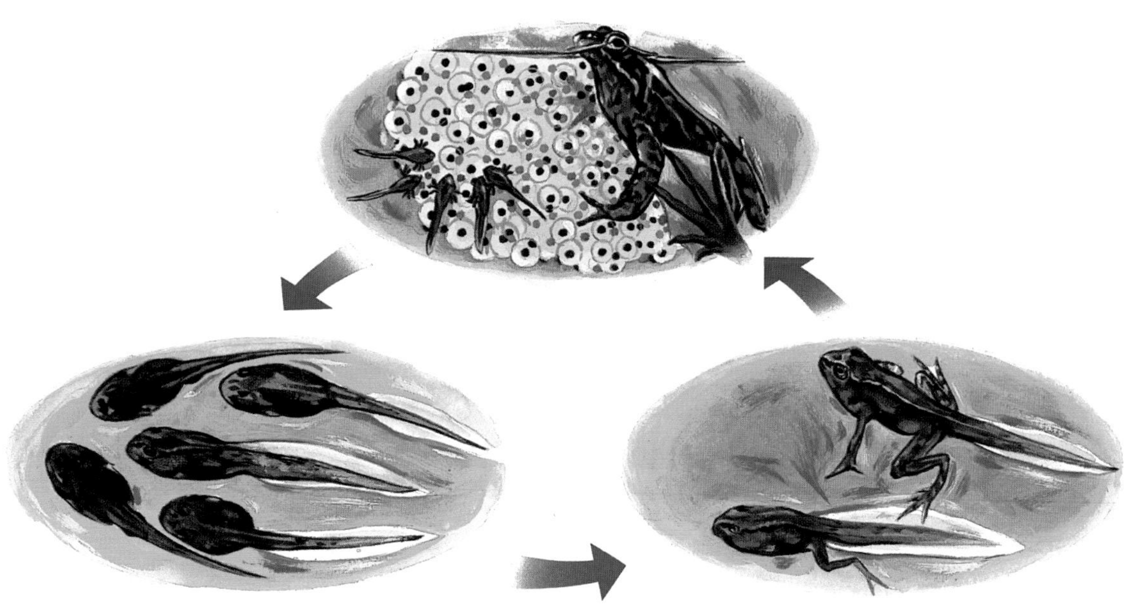

Life cycle of the common frog

Newcomers to Britain

In the past amphibians from other countries have been set free to live in Britain's countryside. They include the edible frog and the marsh frog. But please do not buy the exciting bullfrog tadpoles from North America which some pet shops sell!

Adult bullfrogs do not make easy pets, and it is now against the law to release any animal from abroad into the wild. This is because they sometimes compete with British plants and animals for food and habitats.

British toads and newts

Can you tell toads from frogs? British toads have a rougher, dryer skin than frogs. They move differently too. The common toad crawls along, with an occasional lumpy hop, while the rare natterjack toad scampers about in its heathland home.

Toads

In Spring, toads wake from their winter hibernation and crawl back to their home ponds to mate. The eggs are laid in two rows inside a long string of jelly, which the female twists around water plants. Common toad tadpoles are almost black, but natterjack tadpoles usually have a white patch under their chin.

Common toad

Natterjack spawn is laid in shallow water in sandy places.

Newts

There are three species of newt in Britain: the common newt, the palmate newt and the great crested newt. All three belong to the salamander family. Newts look rather like lizards in shape, but their skins are soft and damp and they move fairly slowly on land. Like frogs and toads, they spend a lot of time out of the water hunting for small creatures to eat.

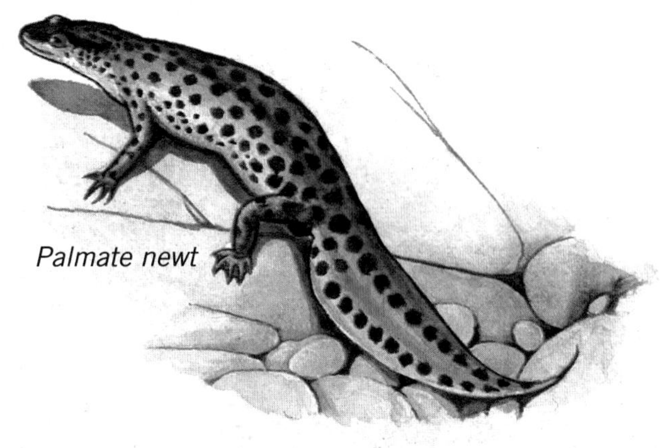

Palmate newt

Great crested newt

The palmate newt is about 7.5 cm long.

The common newt is about 8.5 cm long.

The great crested newt is about 15 cm long.

Male newts dance in front of the females to attract a mate, fanning their smell towards them with their tails. After mating, the female carefully wraps each egg up in the folded leaf of a pond plant. Newt tadpoles grow their front legs first. Their frill of gills can be seen until they become adults.

Hibernation

All British amphibians hibernate in winter. Newts often hide together under stones or logs in quite large numbers. Toads and newts hibernate on land, but male frogs will often spend the winter buried in the mud at the bottom of a pond, taking in oxygen through their special skins.

The male common newt has a spotted skin. He performs a mating dance in front of the female.

Amphibians around the world

Not all amphibians live in ponds or near water. From rainforests to grassy plains, there are amphibians living in different habitats all over the world. Some even bury themselves under the sand in the desert, and can wait years for the rain to come!

Common green tree frog

In Australia people often encourage the common green tree frog to live in their homes as a family friend. Like other tree frogs, they have sucker toes to help them climb.

With these sucker toes, the common green tree frog can climb up windows!

Cane toad

The huge cane toad was introduced to Australia from South America, because farmers thought it would eat insect pests. As the cane toad has no predators in Australia, there are now too many of them, eating useful creatures as well as plant pests. The poisons in a cane toad's skin are so strong that they can kill a dog.

The cane toad will eat most small creatures.

Strawberry poison-dart frog

The strawberry poison-dart frog lives in South America. It uses bromeliad plants as a nursery to look after its young. Bromeliads grow among the branches of rainforest trees, catching rainwater in the special cups made by their leaves. The female frog puts each of its tadpoles in one of these cups. Every few days she comes back to the bromeliad and lays an extra egg in the water for the tadpole to eat.

Poisons from the skin of the strawberry poison-dart frog are used by rainforest people on the tips of their hunting darts.

The colourful skin of the fire salamander warns other animals that it is poisonous.

Fire salamander

The fire salamander lives in Western and Central Europe. During the day it hides in logs and other damp places to keep its skin moist. In olden times, people sometimes saw it coming out from their burning log fires. They called it the fire salamander because they thought it had been born from the flames.

Caecilians

Caecilians are the third group of amphibians. There are many different kinds, but they can only be found in tropical countries. They have no eyes or legs and either live in water or burrow in dead leaves under rainforest trees. It isn't surprising that they are rarely seen!

Reptiles

Reptiles are sometimes called 'cold-blooded' animals. This means that their body temperature is close to the temperature around them. If they need to be warmer, they have to bask in the sunshine. To get cooler, they must hide in the shade.

Reptiles lay their eggs on land. The young hatch out of their papery shells as small versions of their parents.

Reptile skin is covered with rough, dry scales. The scales on the underside of a reptile's body are larger than the ones on its back. Some kinds also have bony shells.

The reptile family has lived on earth for over two hundred million years. There are about five thousand different species alive today. They can be divided into three main groups: tortoises and turtles; crocodiles and alligators; and snakes and lizards.

Sea turtles bury their eggs in the sand at night.

Tortoises and turtles

Tortoises and turtles have upper and lower shells to protect their bodies. They have hard beak-like mouths and no teeth. Although sea turtles live in water, they must come ashore to lay and bury their eggs. Many eggs and young turtles are taken by predators at this time.

Crocodiles and alligators

Crocodiles and alligators have many teeth, and their skin is covered with big hard scales. They lie flat and almost invisible in the water, watching for their prey with only their eyes and nostrils above the surface.

Snakes and lizards

Most snakes and lizards live on land. Their sensitive forked tongues can taste the wind to detect their prey. Some snake species have pits under their eyes which sense the warmth of an animal's body. This tells the snake that food is near.

Although a snake has no legs, it almost 'walks' on its ribs. The ribs are attached in a special way to help the snake grip the ground.

The pit viper gives a poisonous bite to its prey.

Tuatara

The tuatara is a reptile, but it does not fit into any of these three groups. It is a strange lizard-like animal from New Zealand. Its name comes from the Maori language and means 'spine on the back'.

Tuatara

Mind-boggler

The female American alligator sweeps together a nest of plants and mud with her body and tail. She then lays her eggs and watches over them to keep them safe. If the eggs are laid in a part of the nest where the temperature is lower than 30 °C, only females will hatch. If the temperature is more than 34 °C, only males will hatch. When they hatch, she gently carries the young alligators to the water in her mouth.

American alligator with one of her young

British snakes and lizards

You need to be lucky to see a snake or lizard in Britain. They are shy of human beings and will creep away when they sense the vibrations from your footsteps. Snakes and lizards are also hard to spot because their skins are camouflaged to match the places where they live.

Snakes

The adder is Britain's only poisonous snake. Very few people have died from its bite, and it will not harm you if you leave it alone. You may see male adders fighting for females on a dry sunny bank in Spring.

The stronger of these two fighting adders will mate with the female.

Grass snakes often grow to over a metre long. They prefer damp places and can be seen swimming in ponds, where they hunt for frogs and fish. Although the grass snake is harmless, it can leave a bad smell on your skin if you handle it.

Grass snake

The smooth snake lives only in a few places in southern England. It is especially rare because most of the sandy places where it lives have been destroyed to make way for farming or building.

Smooth snake

Lizards

The sand lizard, like the smooth snake, lives on sand dunes and heathland. It is very rare indeed, because of threats to its habitats.

Sand lizard

The common lizard lives in warm dry places throughout Britain. It is the only reptile that lives in Ireland. Unlike most other reptiles, its eggs hatch while still inside the female's body, and the lizards are born alive.

Common lizard

Although the slow worm has no legs, it is still a lizard! It can often be found in country gardens, and especially likes to feed on slugs in warm compost heaps.

Slow worm

Hibernation

When reptiles become very cold, they cannot move quickly to hunt or escape danger. British reptiles hibernate from October to around February to avoid cold weather and shortages of animal prey. Sand lizards dig a burrow for themselves. Other snakes and lizards find a ready-made hole, perhaps under a tree root. While they are hibernating, their body temperature drops and their heart and breathing rate slows down. However, on bright winter days they sometimes wake up to bask in the sunshine.

What is a bird?

From penguins to swallows, from vultures to parrots, there are over nine thousand bird species living in the world today. Although each species is different, they all have certain things in common. They all have feathers, wings and the scaly legs of their reptile ancestors. They also all lay eggs and are warm-blooded. This means that their temperature is controlled by their own body and not by the weather.

The world's largest bird is the ostrich. It measures about 2.5 metres high and lays an egg weighing 1.35 kilograms. Although it cannot fly, the ostrich can run at 48 kilometres per hour, and will fight and kick at any predator that can catch up with it.

The ostrich has huge feet to stop it sinking in the sand.

The smallest bird is the Cuban bee hummingbird, which weighs about as much as six paperclips. Its eggs are less than a centimetre long and are laid in a nest made of spider's webs. It can fly extremely fast, both forwards and backwards, and feeds mainly on high-energy nectar from flowers.

The Cuban bee hummingbird spends most of the day drinking nectar from flowers.

Feathers and flying

Most birds are wonderful flying machines. They have streamlined bodies, wings and keen eyesight. Their bones and beaks are hollow for lightness, and they even have special air-sacs leading from their lungs to hold extra air.

Feathers are shaped like long scales. A magnifying lens will show you that they are more complicated than they look! Each feather is made up of smaller sections, all zipped together by tiny hooks. If the sections are accidentally pulled apart, the bird can stroke them together again by running them through its beak. This is called preening.

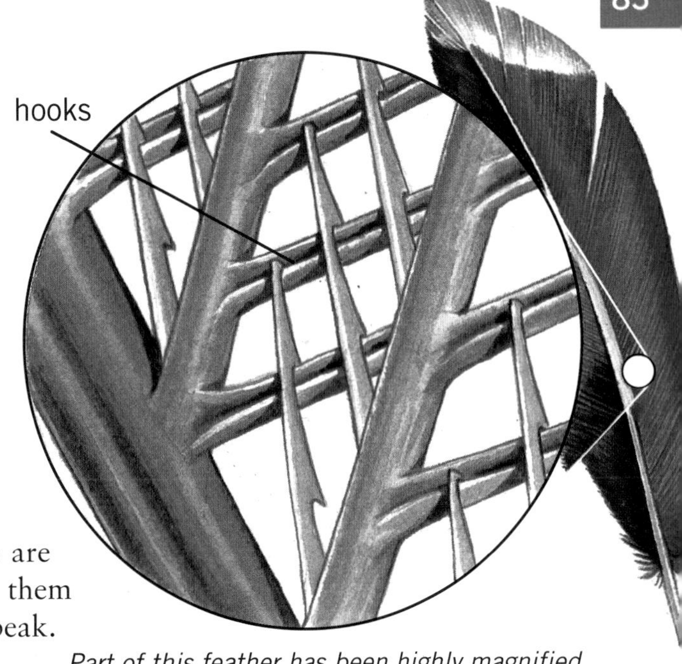

Part of this feather has been highly magnified to show how it hooks together.

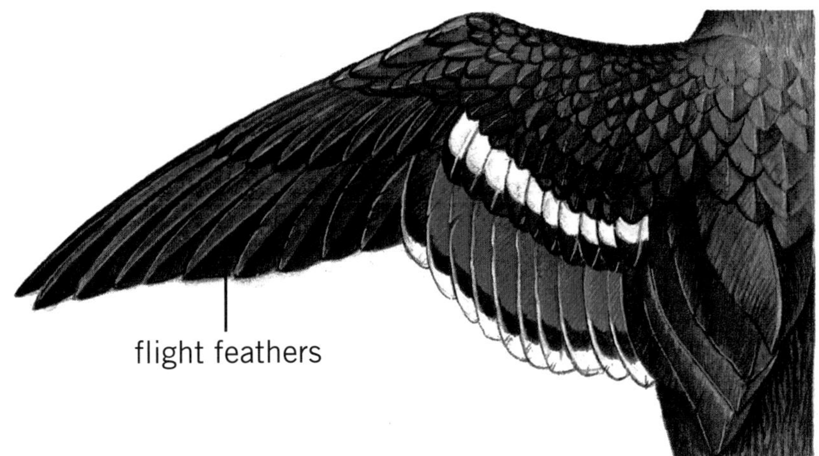

Birds have long stiff flight feathers at the tips of their wings. These push the air down as the bird flies, then open out to let air flow through them as the wings are lifted again.

Watch birds carefully to see how they fly.

Body feathers are waterproof and overlap so that water runs off them when it rains. Under the body feathers are fluffy down feathers for warmth. When a bird puffs its feathers up in cold weather, it is really wrapped in its own built-in quilt!

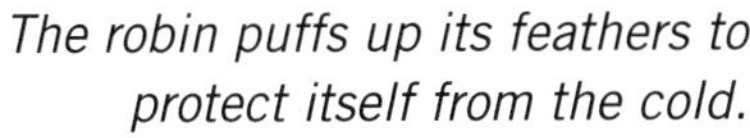

The robin puffs up its feathers to protect itself from the cold.

Bird life cycles

Most birds mate and lay their eggs in Spring. The male attracts the female by offering food or finding a good nesting place, or by performing a special dance called a 'display'.

The male then hops onto the hen's back and sends a liquid full of sperm from his body into the hole under her tail. Some sperm must swim into the egg cells inside her for chicks to begin to grow. A few days after mating, the eggs are ready to be laid.

Great crested grebes perform a mating display.

Chicks from ground nests can run about and feed themselves almost as soon as they hatch, although they still need an adult to guard them.

Chicks from nests in trees and buildings are blind and naked when they hatch. Bluetit parents can bring around five hundred caterpillars to their chicks each day for about seventeen days. Even after the chicks can fly, their parents carry on feeding them for several days, until they are able to hunt for themselves.

This lapwing has made a hole in the ground and laid her camouflaged eggs there.

Adaptations

The shape, appearance and behaviour of animals show how they have adapted to live successfully in their habitats.

The turnstone lives in a beach habitat. Its black-and-white feathers camouflage it against the pebbles. It uses its specially strong bill to turn over stones to find tiny animals to eat.

Turnstones can open mussels with their strong bills.

In open fields it is easy to watch the skylark singing as it hovers high in the sky. But you will not easily spot its nest on the ground, because the skylark's behaviour is adapted to deceive you. It will land quite a long way away from its nest, and then run secretly through the grass stems to reach it.

Ducks are just made for water! Their webbed feet help them to swim, and although they have no teeth, their bills have rough edges for holding wet, slippery food. Ducks also have an extra eyelid, which is clear. This allows them to see underwater. They search for food by tipping upside-down with their tails in the air.

Male ducks are called drakes. Their bright colours attract female ducks.

Migration

It is hard for British birds to find food in winter, although many species manage well on seeds, berries, molluscs and worms. Because insects usually die or hibernate in cold weather, most insect-eating birds take a long flight to a warmer country to find food. This is called migration.

Before migration begins, the birds eat as much as they can to store up extra energy in their body fat. Some even double their weight! Then they flock together and set off on their long journey.

Swallows meet for their long journey south.

Birds find their way over hundreds of kilometres using the sun and the stars. Young birds sometimes migrate later than their parents, but they still know how to find their way.

There are migration flights in all directions. Not all of these journeys are long, but they are all very dangerous and many birds die. Those which survive will return home to lay their eggs in Spring.

Mind-boggler

The Arctic tern makes the longest migration journey of all. Its main food is small fish, but as the Arctic winter draws in, the daylight hunting hours get shorter and shorter. So it flies across the world to the Antarctic. The journey there and back again is about sixty thousand kilometres!

Narrow wings and a trailing tail help the Arctic tern on its long, swift journey across the world.

Watching garden birds

You can help the birds in your garden by offering them food, especially in winter. Birds with short stubby beaks are seed-eaters. They enjoy wet brown bread and other foods made with grains. Those with needle-sharp bills are insect-eaters. They prefer cheese or meat. Experiment with different foods to see which birds prefer which foods. Soon the birds will become quite tame, and you can watch them carefully to find out about bird behaviour!

The chaffinch has a short stubby beak to help it crack seeds.

Bluetits cling to the thinnest twigs as they search for tiny insects. In winter they eat nuts and seeds, sometimes while hanging upside-down.

Noisy gangs of starlings chase each other and squabble over scraps of food. They love to have squawking, splashing parties in the bird-bath!

A male blackbird guards his own part of the garden, threatening other blackbirds which come into his territory. They fight, flying up into the air beak to beak.

Mammals

A mammal is an animal that feeds its young on milk made by the mother's body. Usually, but not always, the babies grow inside the mother. Mammals are warm-blooded animals. Most have four limbs and either hair or fur.

Egg-laying mammals

Egg-laying mammals, such as the echidna and duck-billed platypus, are often called 'primitive mammals'. Their soft-shelled eggs and the way their shoulder bones are joined show that they have evolved from the reptiles.

The duck-billed platypus is very rare and lives only in Australia. Its eggs are laid in a burrow in the bank of a stream. The female curls round the eggs to keep them warm. When they hatch, she feeds the young animals on milk from special glands in her body, although she has no teats.

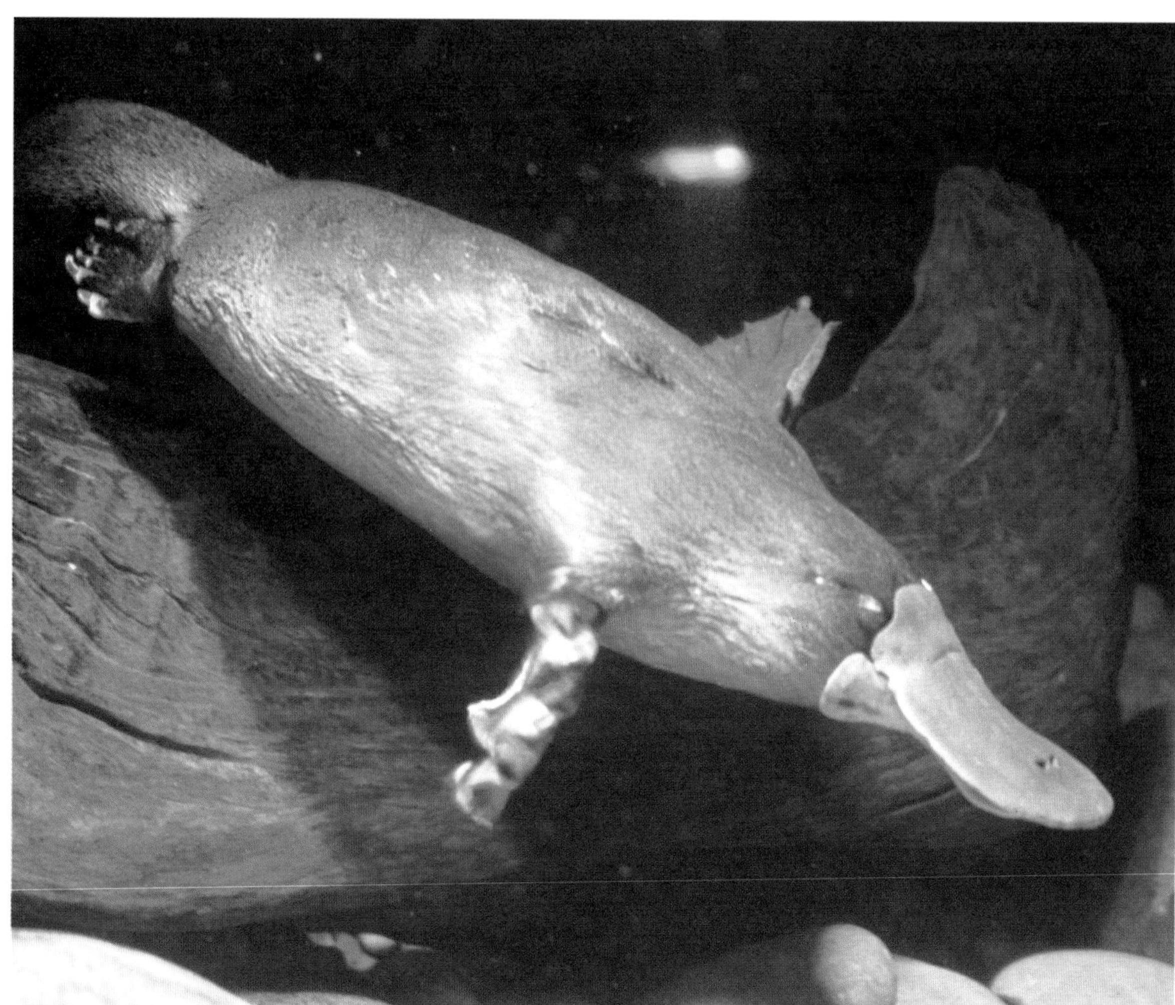

The duck-billed platypus has webbed feet for swimming in rivers.

Pouched mammals

Over fifty million years ago the lands of South America, Antarctica and Australia were all joined together in one huge country. This was the home of pouched mammals, such as the kangaroos and koalas. Then these lands floated apart. The pouched mammals died out in cold Antarctica, and only a few now live in South America. But in Australia and its surrounding islands, they continue to live and thrive!

A newly-born kangaroo is as short as your thumb. Although it is blind and naked, it still manages to crawl through its mother's fur to the safety of her pouch. Inside the pouch is a teat, where the baby can feed until its fur grows and its eyes open.

Kangaroo and joey

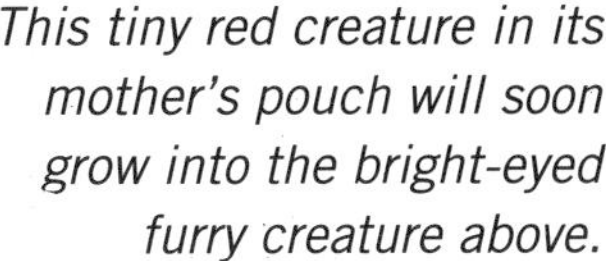

This tiny red creature in its mother's pouch will soon grow into the bright-eyed furry creature above.

A baby elephant is safe under its mother's body.

Placental mammals

This is the largest group of mammals, and includes human beings. The babies of placental mammals grow inside the mother. Some of the oxygen she breathes and the food she eats is passed to the baby dissolved in her blood. Although most placental mammals are helpless when they are born, some can walk within a few hours of birth. But even these still need their mother's care and are fed on milk.

There are around four thousand species of placental mammals scattered all over the world. This book can tell you about only a few of them!

Mammals worldwide

Mammals live all over the world and have adapted to many different habitats. Because they are warm-blooded, their temperature usually stays the same, whether they are panting in the heat or fluffing up their fur in the cold. Some mammals hibernate in winter to survive the cold. Their temperature then drops and their heartbeat slows down.

In the oceans

Whales are perfectly adapted to a life at sea. Their front legs have evolved into strong flippers for swimming. Even their young are born in the water and can swim at once. Their bodies are streamlined and almost fish-shaped, although the tail moves up and down and not from side to side. They have a few bristly hairs, but it is the thick layer of fat under the skin which keeps them warm.

The killer whale has teeth and feeds on animals such as seals and penguins.

The whale's nostrils are at the top of the head. This allows it to breathe easily when it comes up to the surface. Some kinds of whales can stay underwater for as long as an hour.

One group of whales has teeth and feeds on fish and other sea creatures. Dolphins and killer whales belong to this group. Another group, the baleen whales, have a kind of strainer in their mouths instead of teeth. They sieve small creatures, called krill, from the water to eat. This group includes the blue whale, which is the largest animal on earth. The blue whale can measure up to 30 metres long!

The blue whale does not have teeth and feeds on krill.

In the South American rainforests

The three-toed sloth is so closely adapted to tree-top life that it could survive nowhere else. Its claws have evolved into long hooks which cling to the branches as it hangs underneath them. Even its fur grows downwards, in the opposite direction to other animals' coats. In the rainy season, the sloth looks green because tiny plants grow among its hairs.

The three-toed sloth moves slowly. This is because it only eats leaves, and there's no rush to find leaves in a rainforest! It comes to the ground just once a week, to leave its droppings.

A baby sloth travels through the trees clinging to its mother's fur.

The howler monkey's throat acts as a natural loudspeaker.

The howler monkey has solved another difficult rainforest problem. The trees here are so thick that monkey families cannot see each other through the leaves and branches. So the howler monkey has developed a call that can be heard over 3 kilometres away. The call warns other families to keep their distance. It is so like a jaguar's roar that early explorers were terrified when they heard it!

From African plains to farmyard fields

On the plains of Africa survival often depends on mammals living and working together in groups. While lions work together to catch gazelles to eat, the gazelles work together to look out for danger!

On the plains of Africa

Working as a team, sand-coloured female lions chase the plains animals to see which is the slowest and weakest. Once the prey has been chosen, the lionesses hunt without mercy, sometimes driving the animal into an ambush. When they finally catch their prey, they hold it by the nose or throat until it suffocates. The male lions, which are too heavy to hunt well, then push the females aside and eat first.

Herds of gazelles graze the tough grasses, grinding them with their strong back teeth. Their camouflaged coats match the scorched grassland where they live. While they eat, the gazelles scan the plains for predators. Dozens of eyes working together have a better chance of spotting danger. If a chase does begin, they will make zigzag leaps into the air to confuse their pursuers.

Lions hunt zebras and springbuk antelope on the plains of Namibia, Africa.

On the farm

Thousands of years ago, human beings tamed some kinds of plains mammals for use on farms and in their homes. In the eighteenth century, British farmers began carefully choosing which farm animals to mate with one another to produce the best animals for meat, milk or wool. In this way, special breeds of farm animals gradually came into being. They included Jersey cows, Hereford cattle and Cotswold, Leicester and Lincoln sheep.

Hereford cattle were known for their excellent meat and gentle ways.

Jersey cows give rich, creamy milk.

The Lincoln Longwool was prized for its soft wool, which was made into clothes and fabrics.

It is not always easy to see these old breeds on farms today, because British animals are now cross-bred with those from other countries. Charolais cattle have been brought to Britain from France. They add their own special qualities to the old breeds, as they grow more quickly than British cattle and produce leaner meat.

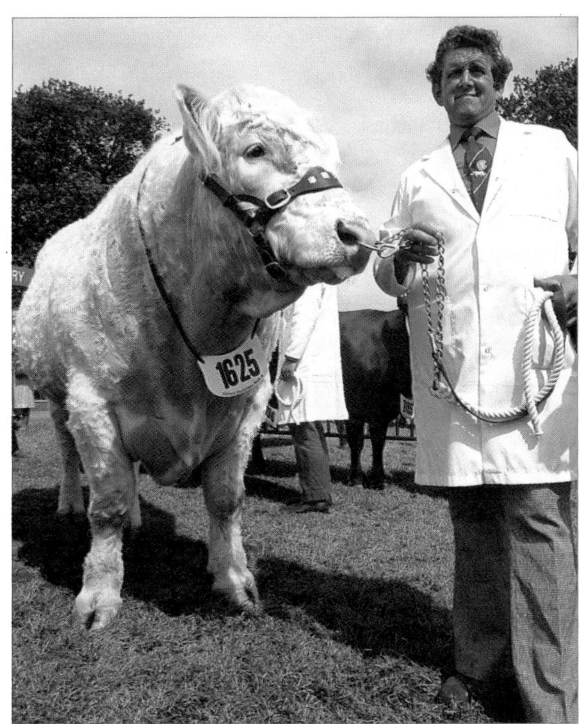

Charolais bull from France

Always, everywhere, some mammals are just kept as special friends.

Mammals and food-webs

There are many mammals in Britain's cool green woods. During the day you can watch squirrels scurrying about, or perhaps disturb a tiny shrew and be surprised at the loudness of its angry chatter! But most of the woodland mammals are nocturnal and come out only at night. They live very secret lives.

Each kind of mammal has its favourite foods. Woodmice, dormice, bank voles and fallow deer mostly eat plants. Bats, moles, shrews and hedgehogs prefer insects or other invertebrates (animals without backbones). Stoats and weasels eat other mammals, while foxes and badgers eat both plants and animals. You can join all the plants and animals in any habitat into a pattern of 'who eats what'. This is called a food-web.

Sometimes food-webs get damaged by natural disasters or by human interference. Stop and think what would happen to the woodland food-web below if the trees were cleared to make way for new houses. What would the plant-eaters do? If the plant-eaters all disappeared, what would happen to the meat-eaters?

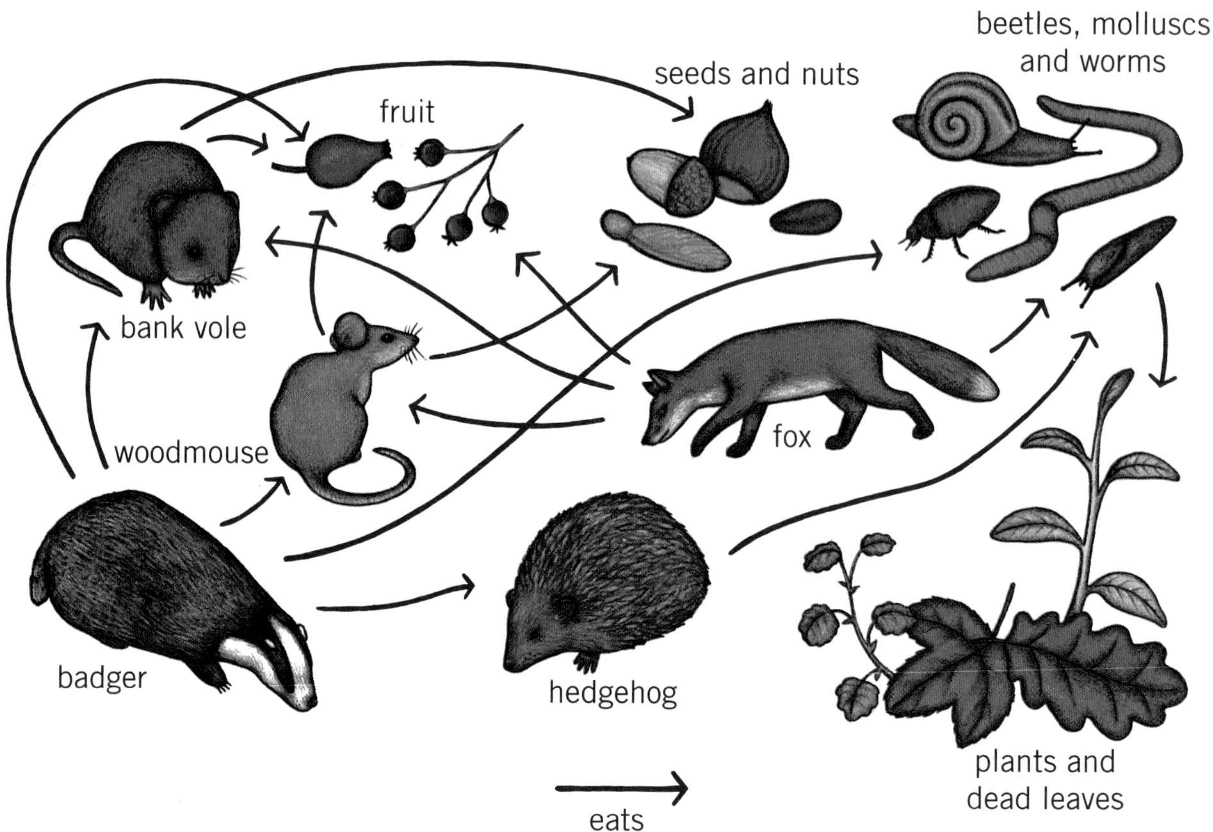

Who eats what in this woodland food-web?

All over the world

In deserts, oceans, rainforests, grassy plains and all other habitats throughout the world, there are food-webs linking together every living thing. People are part of these food-webs, suffering just as much as any other animal or plant if the webs get damaged. But unlike other animals, human beings can decide to help the world's wildlife. They can try not to damage its food-webs and habitats. If you would like to help the animal world, why not write to the clubs below to find out how to join? Please remember to enclose a large stamped addressed envelope.

WATCH,
Royal Society for
Nature Conservation,
The Green,
Witham Park,
Waterside South,
Lincoln LN5 7JR

The Young
Ornithologists' Club,
Royal Society for the
Protection of Birds,
The Lodge,
Sandy,
Beds SG19 2DL

Mute swans nesting in a polluted canal

Children clearing the riverbed of pollution

Take care of the wonderful animal kingdom. It is yours to share and to care.

Published by BBC Educational Publishing, a division of BBC Education, BBC White City, 201 Wood Lane, London W12 7TS

First published in this form 1997

Colour reproduction by Dot Gradations Ltd, England

Acknowledgements

Edited by Caroline White
Designed by Jo Digby
Picture research by Helen Taylor

Illustrations: © John Dunne 1995 (pages 58, 59, 60, 72 and 73); © Martin Knowelden 1995 (pages 63, 66, 80, 81 and 87); © Sean Milne 1995 (pages 53, 55, 57, 65, 68, 6970, 71, 74, 75, 83 and 90); © Sally Olding 1995 (pages 50, 51, 52, 56, 85, 93 and 94)

Photos: Ardea **pp. 53 (John Clegg), 54 (bottom) (Ian Beames), 65 (John Mason), 84 (top) (Jack A. Bailey), 93 (top);** Bruce Colman **Ltd pp. 55, 57, 61 (top and bottom), 66, 67 (bottom), 69, 70, 72, 76 (top), 80, 82 (top), 89 (top and bottom), 92, 93 (bottom);** NHPA **pp. 56, 62, 78, 85, 86 (top), 95;** Oxford Scientific Films **pp. 52, 54, 61 (middle), 64, 67 (top), 76 (bottom), 77, 79 (top and middle), 82 (bottom), 83, 84 (bottom), 86 (bottom), 88, 89 (middle), 91;** Planet Earth pictures **pp. 60, 71, 74, 79 (bottom);** Zefa Pictures **p. 90**

HUMAN BODY

Written by
Steve Pollock

Illustrated by
Salvatore Tomaselli and Claire Bushe

CONTENTS

Inside the human body

There are many systems in the human body which work to keep it going. They all work together and ensure that your body carries on working properly. These systems, which are all working inside you right now, will be covered in more detail in the rest of this book. They are:

The nervous system

The brain is the body's control centre, and messages are sent along nerves which are throughout the whole body.

The endocrine system

Special parts of your body release tiny amounts of chemicals called hormones that control your body chemistry.

The respiratory system

You need oxygen every minute of the day and night, and your lungs are working to keep you alive whether you are asleep or awake.

The skeletal system

Your skeleton protects the soft organs, supports your body and, along with the muscles, helps your body to move.

The excretory system

The kidneys are your waste filtering system. They get rid of most of the waste and pass it out in your urine which is stored in your bladder.

The muscular system

Without muscles, you could never move around. Besides moving the body around, muscles do many other jobs such as moving food along the gut and pumping blood around the body. But muscles can only pull, they never push.

The sensory system

Your senses help you stay in touch with the world. They allow you to experience new things which your brain can store and use in the future. Together, your sense organs and your brain help you learn about and understand the world you live in.

The circulatory system

Your heart pumps blood around your body through the vast network of blood vessels.

The digestive system

This breaks down the food you eat into chemicals which can pass into your body, and then removes any waste.

The reproductive system

These are the parts of the body, different in males and females, which allow us to make more humans.

The lymphatic system

This is the system which helps protect us from infections and diseases.

Find out how all these work as you go through the book.

Making sense of the world

What helps you to know what is going on around you? There are five different senses the human body can use to explore the world. These are: seeing, hearing, touching, tasting and smelling.

For humans to use these senses, a special part of the body is used. These are the sense organs: your eyes, ears, skin, tongue and nose.

Sense organs only collect information – they cannot make sense of it. They receive information and pass it on to the brain along your nervous system as electrical signals. As you grow older, the sense organs help you learn about the world. Each time something new happens, your brain stores the event so that you know what to do next time. All the sense organs are connected to the brain by nerves.

Think about the senses that you would use and what might happen when something rather tasty is cooking in the kitchen.

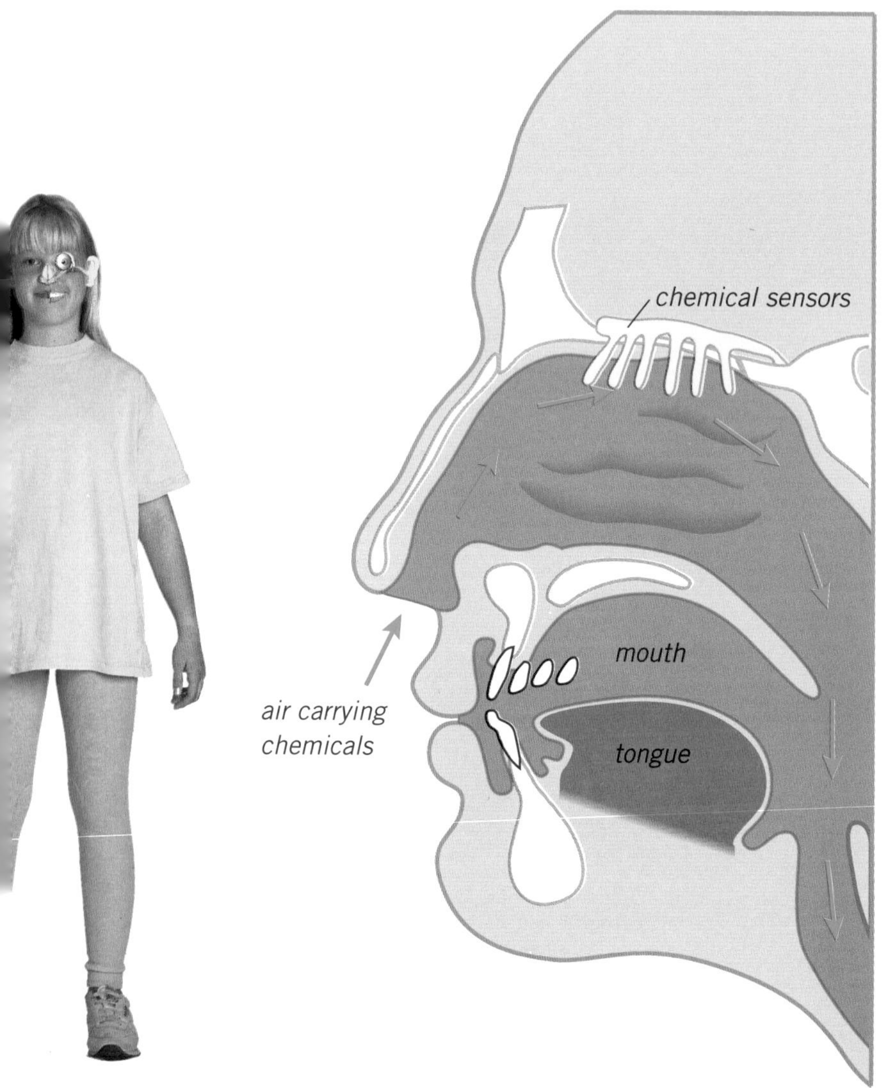

Smelling

Before you get to the kitchen, what sense is telling you that something is cooking? Heating up food releases chemicals as vapour which reach your nose. These stimulate the chemical sensors at the back of your nose, sending messages to your brain. After a time, the smell doesn't seem as strong as the first time you smelt it. It is really but there is no need for your brain to keep reminding you. It is a bit like someone shouting at you to get your attention. Once you are listening, they talk to you in an ordinary voice.

Hearing

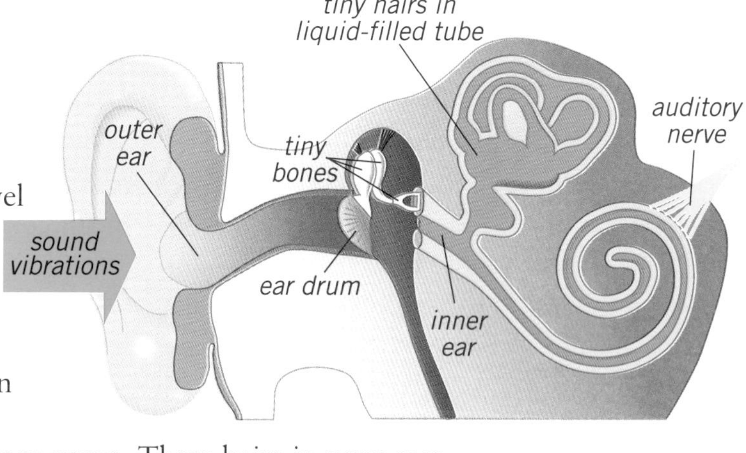

You might then hear the bubbling noises of the cooking. Sound is produced by vibrations which travel through the air. Your outer ear picks up the sound vibrations. These pass into the ear vibrating first the ear drum, then three tiny bones and finally some tiny hairs in a liquid filled tube which send messages to the brain via the auditory nerve. These hairs in your ears help you keep your balance. When you spin around, the liquid in your ears moves fast over the hairs which confuses your brain and makes you feel dizzy.

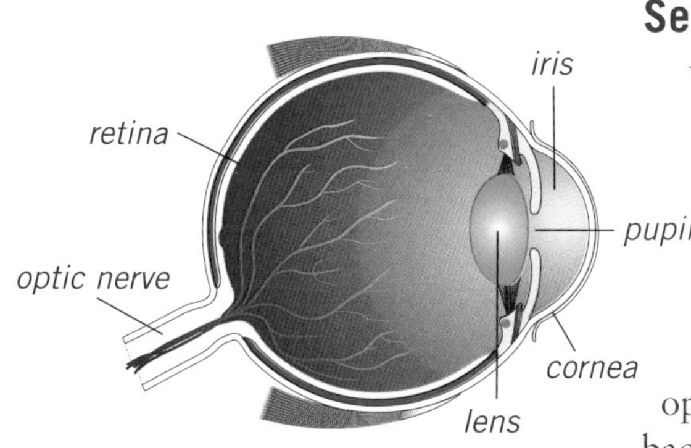

Seeing

When you are close to the pan you may see the steam rising. Your eye works by letting light in through the black centre (your pupils), then through a lens which makes the picture sharp. This picture lands on the back of the inside of the eye, called the retina. The optic nerve sends the picture on the retina back to the brain.

Touching

Getting close to the pan is dangerous. Your brain receives the heat signal from your skin. You feel the heat from the cooker. You are careful about the way you handle the pan. The skin on your hands is sensitive to touch. As you lift off the pan to pour out the food, all your senses and what you have learnt about hot things work together to make sure that you do not spill the hot food.

Tasting

Finally, when you eat the food, your senses of smell and taste are working. Your saliva or spit mixes with the food and helps spread the chemicals which give the food its taste over your tongue. Tastebuds on your tongue test the food for four main tastes – bitter, sweet, sour and salty. The messages are then passed from the tastebuds to the brain.

As we all need food and water to live, this is probably what made you become interested in the food in the beginning!

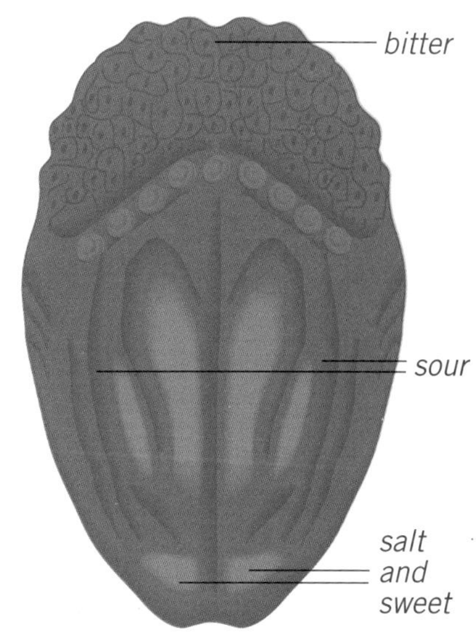

The nervous system

The human brain is connected to a spinal cord and then to a whole network of nerves. These nerves pass from the spinal cord through the whole body. This is the body's nervous system. The brain is the control unit which receives and sends messages through the nerves. The messages are sent as tiny electrical currents which can pass along the nerves very fast. Fast enough to cover the length of a football pitch in one second! The brain contains 10 000 million nerve cells.

The brain does a whole range of different jobs. It keeps the body working all the time, and it supplies every part with food and oxygen. When changes happen outside, the brain makes sure the body reacts to the changes so no harm comes to it. Your brain will do things which can take you by surprise. For example, when you touch something hot you will pull your hand away without having to think about it. When this happens, your brain has avoided the normal nerve channels. This stops you from hurting yourself.

No control

There are other things that happen without you having any direct control. For example, when the light is bright, the pupil in your eye becomes smaller. This makes sure that light sensitive cells inside your eyes are not damaged.

This just happens and there is nothing you can do to control it. These things are controlled by the autonomic nervous system which keeps your heart beating and keeps you breathing, even when you are asleep at night.

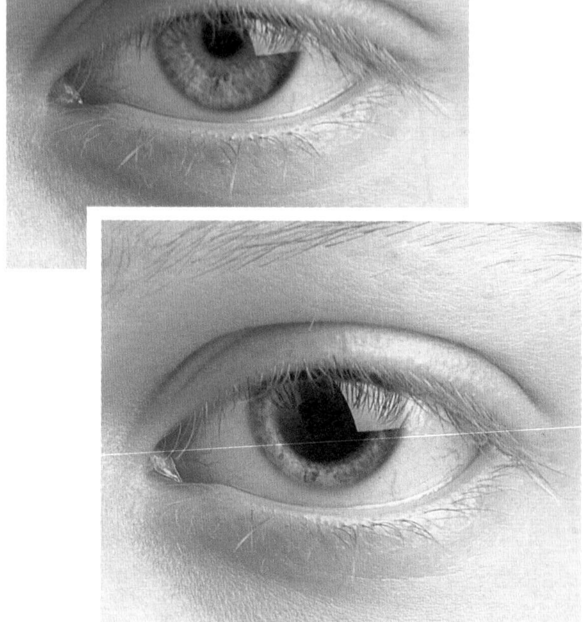

The pupil is small in bright light (above) and much bigger in dim light (below).

Thinking, hearing, speaking

Different parts of your brain control different things. Your brain is split up into three areas responsible for different aspects of your behaviour. These are the sensory cortex, the association areas and the motor cortex.

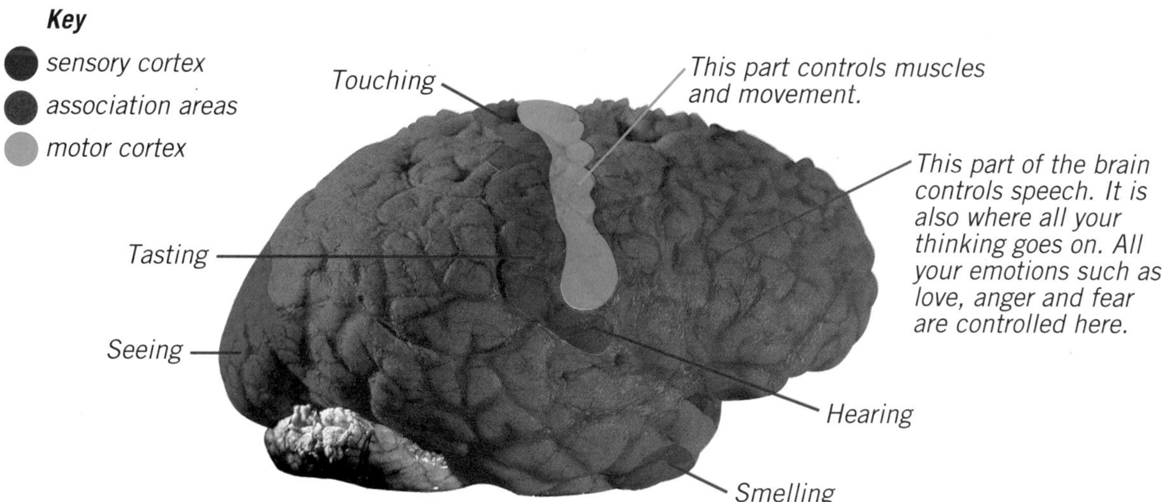

The nerves

These messages are sent through the network of nerves, which are found all through your body. There are two main sorts of nerves. Sensory nerves work by taking messages (tiny electrical impulses) from the body through to the spinal cord and the brain. The brain makes sense of the message. If it needs to act, it sends a message back through different nerves (the motor nerves), to other parts of the body. All this happens very quickly and enables us to respond to the events going on around us.

What a nerve!

You can test some other things that your nervous system can do. Sit on a chair with one leg crossed over another. Use the edge of a ruler or book and tap just under your knee cap. The lower part of your leg will jerk up suddenly. This is known as a reflex action and it is your autonomic nervous system in control.

Skeletons and joints

The reason why your body does not flop all over the place is because there is a skeleton inside you. The bones do the same job as a clothes hanger does for a coat. Without the hanger, the coat is floppy. So the bones in a skeleton support and carry the weight of your body.

The 206 bones in a human body do two other jobs. They protect certain soft parts of the body. For example, the nerves which make up the spinal cord are all protected by many small bones. Together, these make up the backbone. The skull protects the brain, and the ribs protect the heart and the lungs. These parts of the body are very important for keeping you alive and so need extra special protection.

What is bone?

Bone is alive. It is made from strong bendy stuff called cartilage and a hard chalky chemical which gets added to the cartilage as you grow. The older you are, the more brittle the bone gets and the more easily it gets broken. There is still cartilage without any hard stuff in it – in your nose and ears. So the bone is a hollow tube which gives it extra strength. It is also strong yet light because of its honeycomb structure.

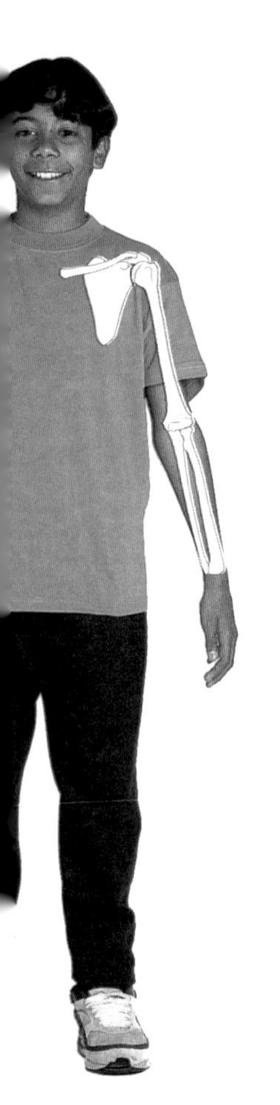

The centre of many bones is filled with a soft material called marrow. It is this part of the bone which is used to make new blood cells. There is also a layer of skin around the bone called the periosteum. This keeps the bone growing whilst it is young or when it needs to mend if it gets broken (see page 105).

air spaces make the bone light

hard bone gives the bone strength

periosteum (layer of skin)

in a living bone, bone marrow is found here

This is a cross-section of a femur (thigh bone).

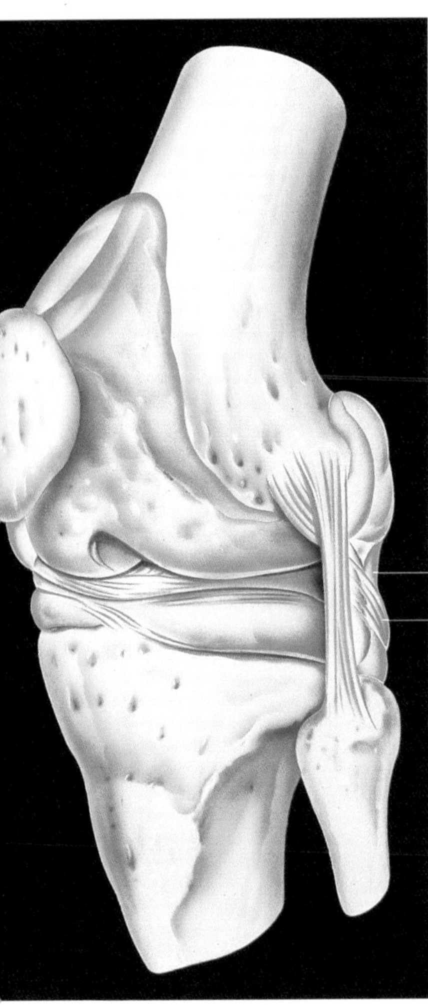

The knee joint is the largest joint in the body.

Joints

The other thing bones allow you to do is move. Whenever two bones meet, they form a joint. Some joints move, others do not. The end of the joint is covered with protective cartilage. The two ends of the bones are joined together with straps called ligaments. These are attached to the bone and can move easily. The joint is covered with synovial fluid which acts like oil to keep the joints smooth. This helps the bone to move easily.

There are two main kinds of joints. The hinge joint which is in the elbows and knees, and the ball and socket joint which is in the shoulders and hips.

Broken bones

Bones can get broken. But because the bones inside us are living material, they can mend. This happens when the cracks in the broken bone grow over with new bone. The broken bone is held rigid in a plaster cast until it mends to make sure that the bone grows properly.

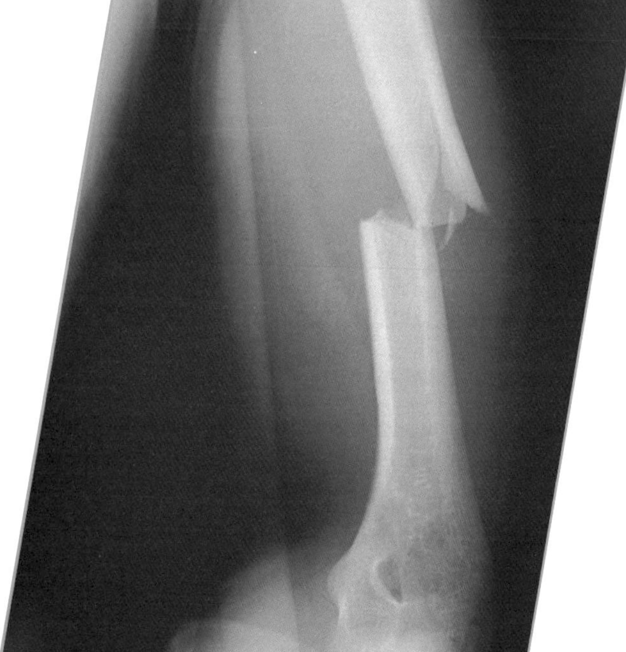

A broken bone in the upper arm (humerus) caused by sudden injury.

Muscles and movement

The skeleton supports the body but it is muscles which help to move the body. If you eat the meat from a cooked chicken or a lamb chop, or any cooked animal, you are eating the animal's muscle. So muscle is meat.

There are different types of muscle. The different jobs these muscles do means they are different in the way they are made up.

Muscles can only pull. None can push. There has to be two muscles to make your arm move. One to pull in one direction, the other to pull in the opposite direction. To bend your arm one muscle tenses, the other relaxes. To move it back to the first position, the relaxed muscle must now tense and the other one relaxes. Nearly all muscles have to work in this way. They work antagonistically. That simply means they work against each other.

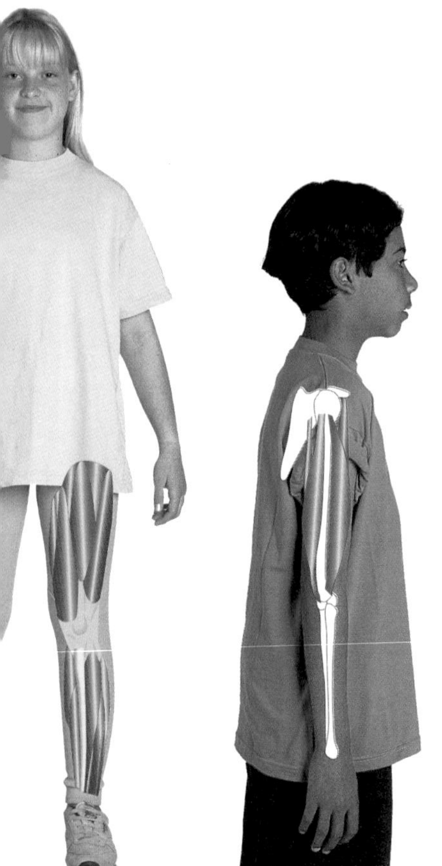

Voluntary muscles

The big muscles in your body are those in your legs, buttocks and arms. They are known as skeletal muscles or voluntary muscles, because we decide when they work. For example, we know when we want to walk. So the muscle only works when we want it to.

Voluntary muscles are made up of bundles of overlapping tiny fibres. When you dangle your arm at your side, the muscle is at rest and the fibres are all relaxed. This makes the muscle long and thin. When you bend your forearm up, the muscle tenses. The overlapping fibres slide over each other and make a thick, fat, short muscle in the upper arm.

Involuntary muscles

When we swallow food, there are muscles working inside us to push the food down into the stomach. When the food is in the stomach, itself a muscular bag, it starts to twist and turn to churn up the food inside. These muscles are known as involuntary muscles because they work whether we like it or not. We have no control over them.

Heart muscles

Then there are the muscles in the heart. These are working every minute of the day, throughout your life, whether you are asleep or awake. The muscles in your heart have a structure that makes sure they never tire, which is just as well!

Fascinating fact

It takes 15 different muscles in our face to make a smile, and we use 200 muscles whenever we take a step!

Tendons

Muscles are joined to the bones they move by tendons. These tendons are flexible straps that pull the bones when the muscles contract. For example, there are no muscles in our fingers, only tendons. So when we move our fingers it is muscles in our arms which pull the tendons, which in turn pull the fingers into the positions we want.

Exercising muscles

It is only exercise which keeps muscles healthy. Increase the amount of exercise and you increase the number of fibres in muscle. When a muscle stops working, for example, when an arm is in plaster, the muscle becomes weak because there are fewer fibres. The number of fibres increases as soon as the muscle starts being exercised again. It is important to have regular exercise to maintain your fitness (see pages 140–1).

How fast can a human body run?

The fastest male runners can finish the 100 metre sprint in under 10 seconds. That is a speed of 36 km per hour. The 100 metres is the fastest race, but the marathon is the longest at 42.2 km. The fastest runners in a marathon can travel at an average speed of 20 km per hour over this long distance.

A breath of fresh air

Breathing is something you do most of the time without having to think about it. The time you most notice it is when you are running and your body is making you breathe extra fast. The reason for breathing faster is that your body needs extra oxygen to keep going.

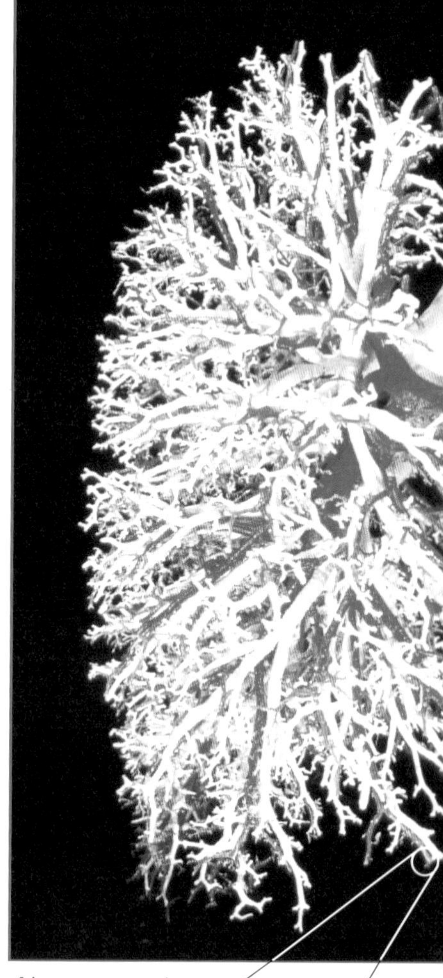

Oxygen is the gas that our bodies use to get the energy from the food we eat. Without oxygen or food, we would very soon die. So when we run fast or do a lot of exercise, we need even more of that oxygen than normal. Each time we get energy from our food we make waste materials, including a gas called carbon dioxide. So breathing is the way we bring oxygen into our bodies and get rid of the carbon dioxide which has built up inside us.

The lungs

You breathe by taking air into your body through your nose and mouth. The air travels down into a tube called a trachea which splits into two tubes called bronchi, one for each lung. Inside the lung, the bronchi split up into more and more smaller tubes called bronchioles. At the end of the bronchioles are tiny sacs called alveoli. Here, the blood vessels are so thin that oxygen from the air in the lungs can pass straight into the blood. At the same time, the carbon dioxide in the blood can pass directly out of the blood into the lungs. A huge area inside the lungs allows for all this swapping of gases to happen.

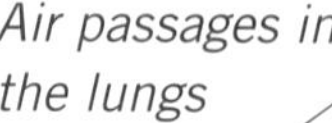

Air passages in the lungs

It is estimated that if the alveoli in a lung were flattened out, they would cover an area the size of a tennis court!

The lungs are made up of a mixture of tiny blood vessels and tubes for carrying air. They are rather soft and look spongy, but they are elastic too because they go up and down when you breathe.

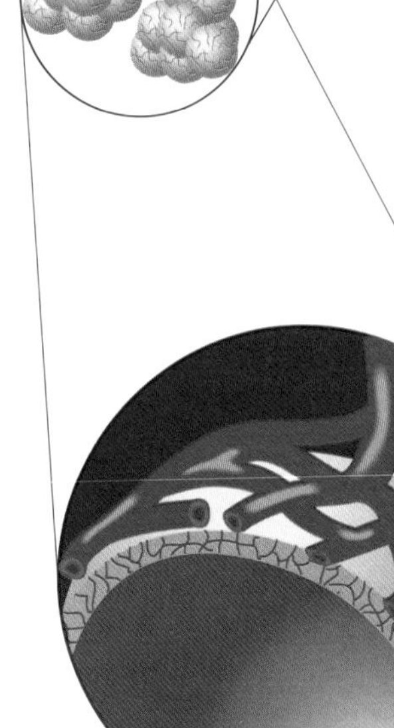

The alveoli. Oxygen passes through the blood vessels and into the blood.

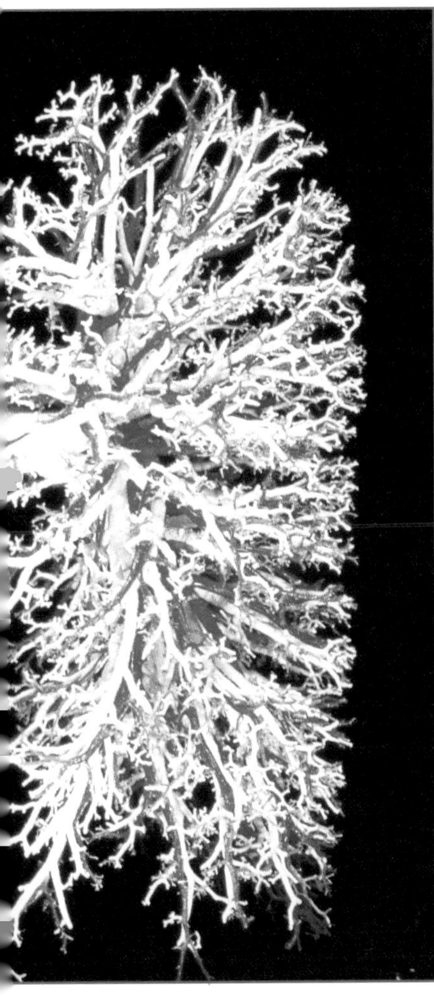

How do we breathe?

Your lungs lie in an airtight box formed by the ribs and the muscles which join them together, and a sheet of muscle called the diaphragm. There is a reason for the box to be airtight. As you breathe in, the muscles between the ribs push the ribs up and out. This causes the diaphragm to pull down and make the space in the box bigger (**1**). Air rushes into the lungs because of this extra space in the box. This makes them inflate like a pair of balloons, filling the extra space made in the airtight box with air. If the box was not airtight, this would not work. When you breathe out, the ribs move down and in and the diaphragm relaxes, pushing up into the box (**2**).

Both these movements reduce the amount of space in the box and the lungs get smaller, forcing air out through the mouth. Part of your brain controls this without you ever having to think about it (see page 103).

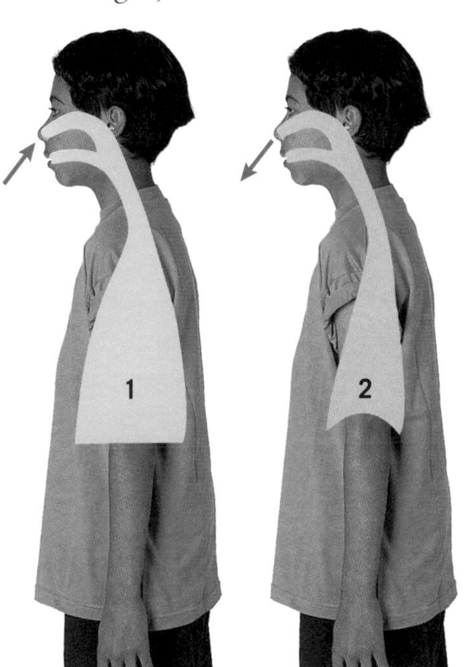

Breathe in, breathe out

Puffing trick

Here's a trick which will fool some people. Push a deflated balloon into an empty, plastic fizzy drink bottle. Make sure you stretch the open end of the balloon over the bottle's open mouth. Ask your friends to try and blow the balloon up. It is impossible because the bottle is filled with air. No matter how hard you blow into the balloon, the air in the bottle stops it from inflating.

Fascinating fact

What are hiccups? These happen when the muscle that controls your breathing (the diaphragm) moves suddenly and makes you gasp.

Heart and circulation

Inside your body is a system of tubes, called blood vessels, which carry blood around your body. There are three types of blood vessels: arteries, veins and capillaries. Blood in arteries carries food and oxygen to where it is needed. These arteries split up into smaller and smaller vessels called capillaries so that blood can get right into every part of our bodies.

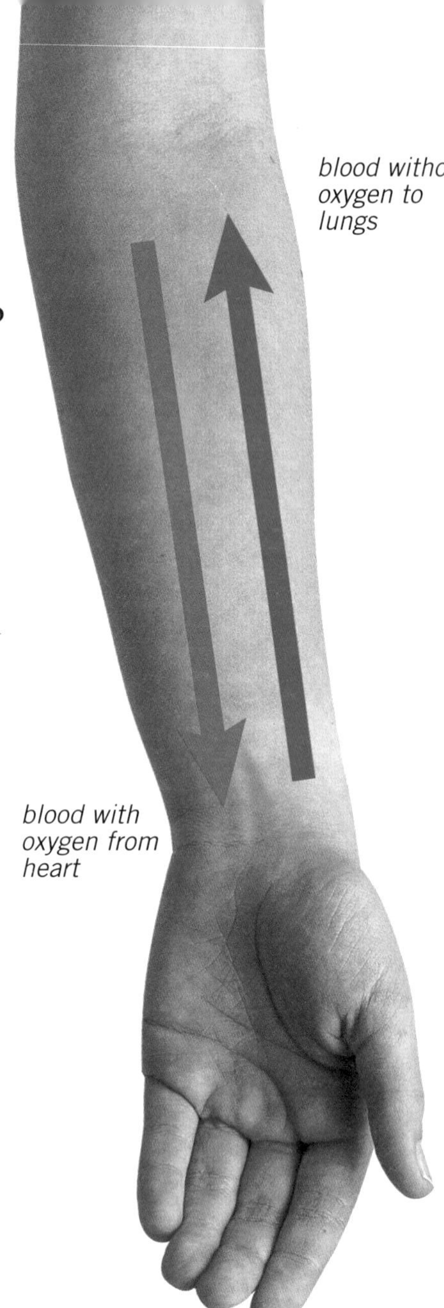

These capillaries mix with the capillaries of other blood vessels called veins. This means that any waste materials such as carbon dioxide (a gas that we produce and need to get rid of) can be taken away by the blood in the veins. The veins then take the blood back into the heart.

Your heart is the pump that keeps the blood flowing around your body. The blood goes from your heart to your lungs before it goes anywhere else in your body. At the lungs, the blood gets rid of any carbon dioxide which can be breathed out. At the same time, the blood picks up oxygen and returns to the heart, ready for its journey around the rest of the body.

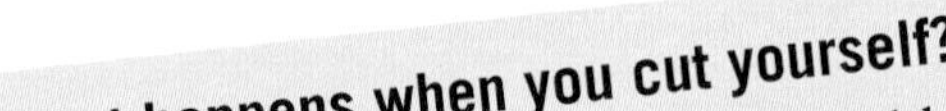

What happens when you cut yourself?

If you cut yourself, your body quickly starts to heal the wound. This happens when blood leaks out of the cut, cleaning the wound. The bleeding stops as soon as the platelets clot the blood which seals up the cut in your skin. This hardens and forms a scab and new skin grows underneath. The scab drops off and after a time you will not remember where the cut was.

How the heart works

To make all this happen, your heart beats 100 000 times each day and a healthy heart never gets tired. A heart is divided into two halves. Both halves each have chambers – an atrium at the top, and a ventricle below.

Blood enters the right atrium, is passed into the right ventricle and then off to the lungs. Blood returning from the lungs enters the left atrium, then the left ventricle and then off around the body.

Valves are found in the veins. These make sure that the blood keeps moving in one direction only. This avoids mixing up blood carrying carbon dioxide with blood carrying oxygen.

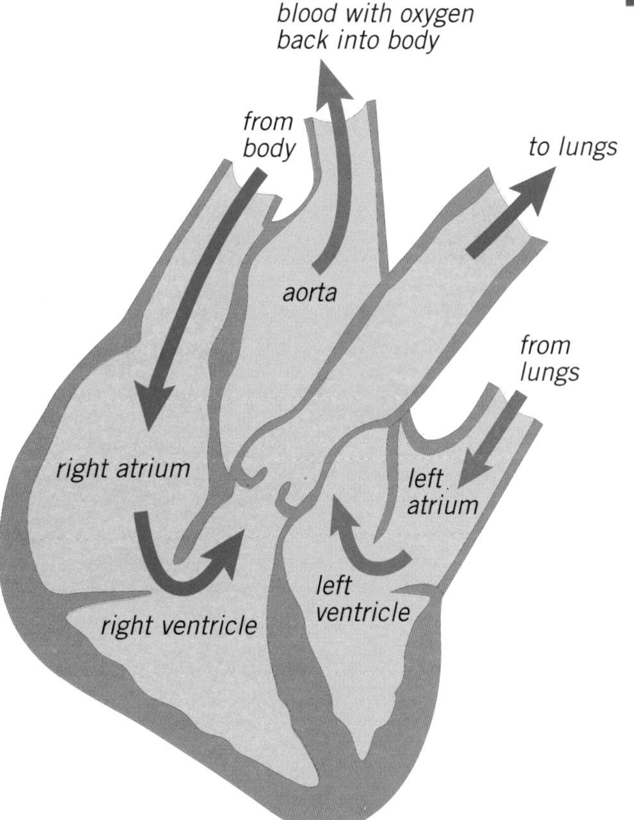

What is blood made of?

Blood is made up of several different things. It is made up of plasma, red blood cells, white blood cells and platelets.

Most of your blood is plasma which is mainly water. Then there are the red blood cells. These carry oxygen around in the blood. To get oxygen, you need iron in your food which you can get from eating vegetables and red meat. There are about 200 million red blood cells in a drop of blood, but every minute you make 140 million new ones. The white blood cells eat bacteria and help fight off diseases. Finally, platelets cause the blood to clot and stop it leaking out when you cut or damage yourself (see page 110).

Other substances are mixed in with the blood. Food that you have eaten is turned into chemicals and dissolved into the water in the blood.

Red and white blood cells with platelets (blue)

Waste disposal

The very act of staying alive makes chemicals which are poisonous to us. When we breathe air, or when we eat anything, a chemical reaction takes place which keeps us alive. But at the same time, new chemicals are made that would kill us if we did not get rid of them. This is what the kidneys are for. They are the body's main filter system, taking out the waste material from the blood.

The process of removing poisons from the body is known as excretion. The kidneys are the main organs of excretion but there are other parts of the body which remove waste as well. These are the liver, the lungs and the sweat glands.

The kidneys

You have two kidneys, situated at either side of the bottom of your spine. They are the same shape as kidney beans, but they are much larger – about the size of your clenched fist.

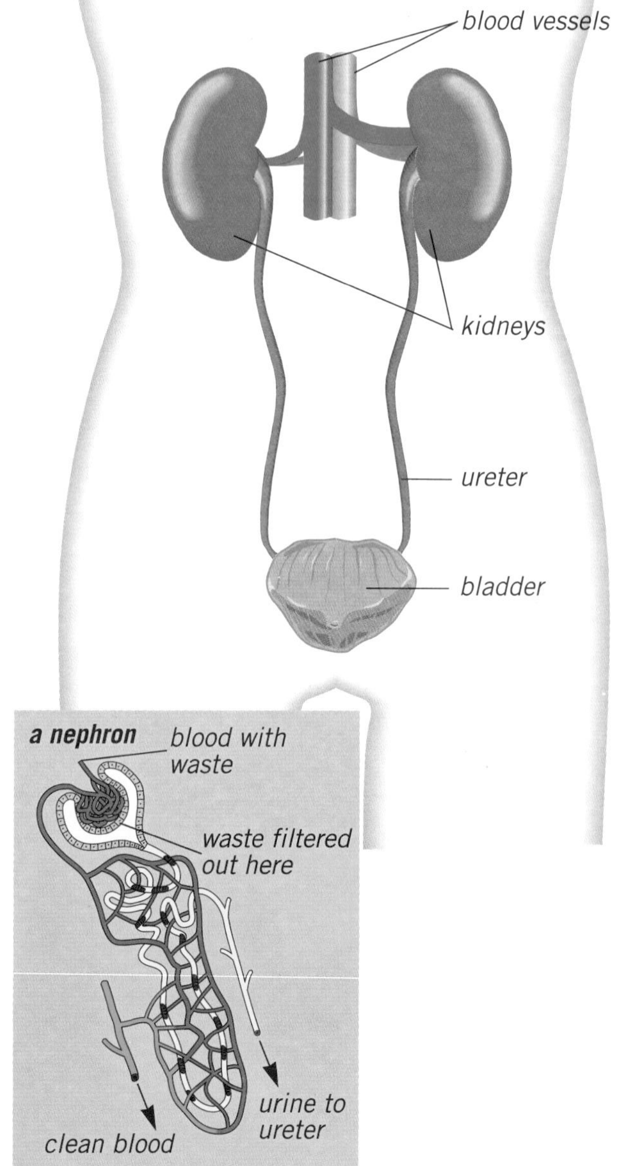

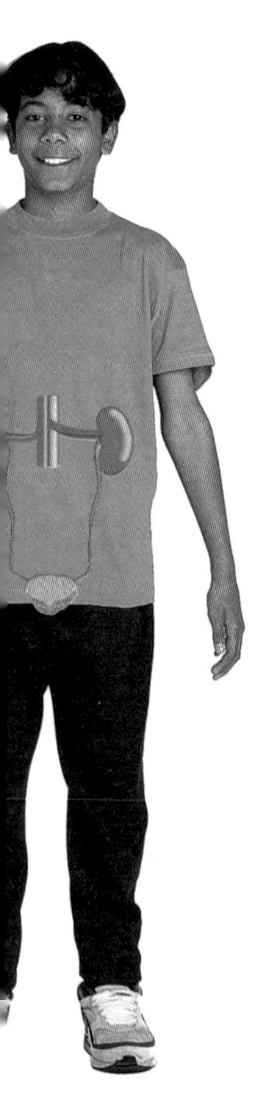

The kidneys filter out the waste chemicals in the blood and remove any water the body does not need. The waste chemicals and the water are passed out of your body as urine. Kidneys are important as they keep the water balance of the body just right. For example, on hot days when you have lost a lot of water through sweating, there may not be much water in your urine. The urine will be dark yellow because there are a lot of waste chemicals and not much water.

Inside the kidneys are millions of tiny filtering units called nephrons that do the work. Unfiltered blood, containing waste material, is brought to the kidney in the renal artery and passes into the nephrons. It gets separated and clean blood is passed back into the body in the renal vein, and urine passes into the ureter.

The bladder

The ureters are long tubes which come out of the kidneys and pass into the bladder where urine is stored. When the bladder is full, it is ready to be emptied. This is what happens when we go to the toilct.

Losing water

Seventy per cent of our bodies is made up of water and we lose 3 litres of water each day. There are three main ways of losing water: through the skin by sweating, through our breath when we breathe and by excretion in our urine. But the kidneys play an important role in making sure the salt and water balance in our bodies is right. This is done through hormones (see pages 122–3). These are special chemical messengers which are released into the blood when the water level is too low or too high.

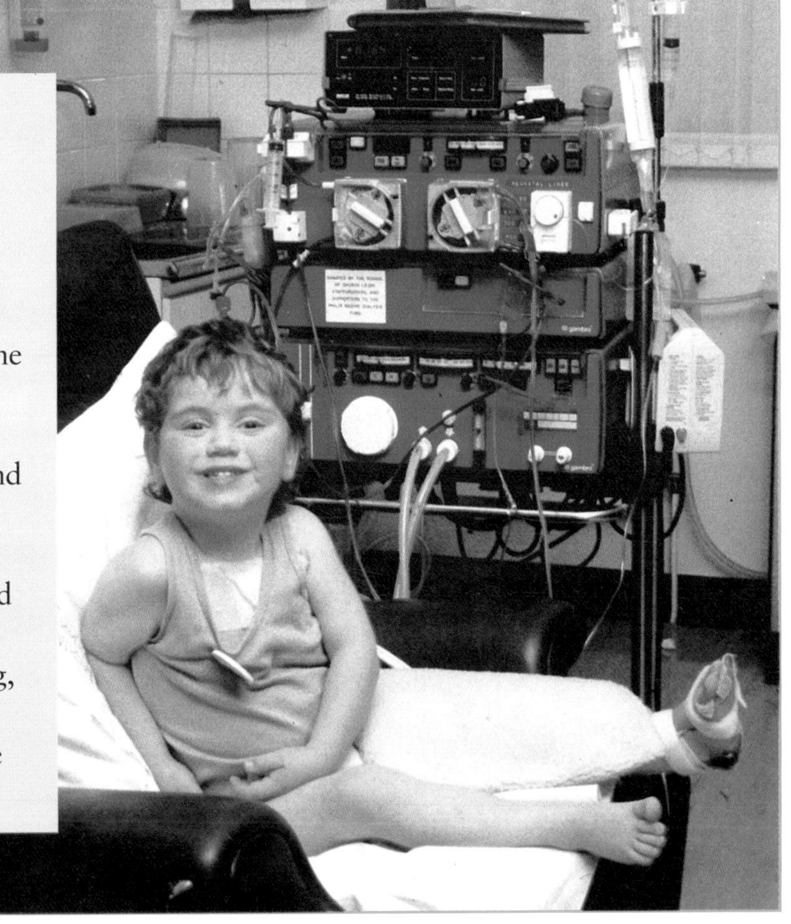

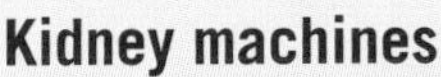

Kidney machines

Some people have only one kidney. Others may suffer from kidney disease. These people have to have the poisons in their body removed by a special machine called a dialysis machine. Their blood supply is connected to the machine and it acts in the same way as a kidney. It filters out the poisons and puts clean blood back into the person's body. If the kidneys need replacing, it is even possible to transplant kidneys from one person to another.

A day in your life

Your body goes through changes everyday. Whatever happens to you during each day, your body works hard to keep you well and comfortable. If you are healthy but become unwell, your body stands a chance of fighting any diseases. If you are unhealthy and unwell, then your body has a more difficult job to do.

Throughout each day, different things are happening in your body without you really noticing them. All these help to keep you feeling well.

Fast asleep

When you are asleep your heartbeat, breathing and body temperature level is low. You are using hardly any energy. All your muscles are relaxed. Your body is very still, so there is no need to for it to be working hard. That would be a waste of your body's energy.

Back at home

Now your body must recover by resting. You eat a meal and drink to boost your energy and fluid levels. You relax, your heartrate and breathing lower and your body is getting ready for rest. When you are in bed, your whole body slows right down. This gives your body a chance to make new cells to repair any damage to your body and fight infection.

Play sport

Playing sport will put your body through many changes. You will need a surge of energy to keep you running around on the games field. Heart rate and breathing will be high. Your body will be getting hot because of all the energy that you are using. Sweating takes the heat away from the body as it evaporates. As you play harder, you damage a part of your body. You don't notice at first. Your body deals with it by releasing adrenaline into your blood. Your lungs let in more air, and your heart pumps more blood to your muscles. Food stored in your liver is released to give more fuel to your muscles, and your skin turns pale because blood is sent from there to your muscles too. You sweat more too to keep the muscles cooled down.

Wake up!

When you first get up, your body has to make sure that your heartbeat, temperature and breathing rates all go up. For this to happen, your body needs more oxygen passing around it. You need to operate at the right temperature if all the chemical reactions going on in your body can take place. Your body is performing thousands of chemical experiments and these all happen best at a certain temperature – 37 degrees centigrade. You have a natural energy store from the food you ate the day before. This gives you the energy you need to get going. You also need to get rid of the waste that has built up in your body overnight, so you go to the toilet to empty your bladder.

Have breakfast

Breakfast is the first chance to get more energy into your body. You drink and eat food which is digested to give you the energy that you need to carry on through the day.

Walk to school

This is the first time today that your body is really using up energy. Your muscles need oxygen and they also need food. So your heart rate and your breathing rate both go up. You might be late and run some of the way, so you feel yourself sweating. Your body is losing some of the water that you drank at breakfast time to stop your body from overheating. When you get to school you will have to get a drink to replace the water your body has lost.

Sit in class

Now you are sitting still in class, both your heartbeat and your breathing rate have fallen. Your body needs less energy now because it is not moving around much. But as the morning goes on, you begin to feel hungry. This means you need more energy to keep your body temperature at a steady level. You go off to lunch and the level of sugar in your blood rises giving you energy. The hormone called insulin is produced to control the level of sugar in your blood and to make sure that just the right amount is released.

Nutrition and healthy eating

There is an expression, "You are what you eat." The food you eat contains the chemicals which will become part of your body. As you grow, particularly from a baby into a child, your body needs different foods to do different jobs. For example, you need calcium to make bones grow. Eat the right kind of food and your body has every chance of being healthy. Eat the wrong kind of food and you could make yourself unhealthy, or even get diseases.

When people talk about eating a balanced diet, they mean eating a variety of different foods containing nutrients (see below). Make sure you eat a mix of foods to give you a balanced diet. Good food, such as fresh fruit and vegetables, helps to balance out food which is not so good for you, such as chips or chocolate. If you ate only the chips or chocolate, you would very quickly become unhealthy.

Energy

The food you eat has an energy value. On food packet labels it can be seen as kilojoules or kilocalories. So 100 grams of cereal is 1550 kj. A 100 grams of yoghurt is 220 kj. The first is very rich in energy, the second is less so. Different kinds of foods have different energy values. Food gives you the energy to stay alive and you depend on this.

Different kinds of people have different energy needs. A 12 to 14-year-old boy needs 11 000 kj, but a girl of the same age needs 9000 kj. If you spent your day running around, you would need more food than if you sat at a desk all day. But eating food isn't just about getting energy to live. Your body needs several different kinds of food, containing a variety of nutrients, if you are to stay healthy.

NUTRITION INFORMATION per 100g

ENERGY	kj	1550
	kcal	370
PROTEIN	g	15
CARBOHYDRATE	g	75
(of which sugars)	g	(15)
(starch)	g	(60)
FAT	g	1.0
(of which saturates)	g	(0.5)
FIBRE	g	2.5
SODIUM	g	0.9
VITAMINS:		(% RDA)*
VITAMIN C	mg	100 (165)
VITAMIN D	mg	8.3 (165)
THIAMIN (B_1)	mg	2.3 (165)
RIBOFLAVIN (B_2)	mg	2.7 (165)
NIACIN	mg	30 (165)
VITAMIN B_6	mg	3.3 (165)
FOLIC ACID	mg	333 (165)
VITAMIN B_{12}	mg	1.7 (165)
IRON	mg	23.3 (165)

* Recommended Daily Allowance

NUTRITION INFORMATION
100 g provides
ENERGY 220 kj/52 kcal
PROTEIN 4.6 g
CARBOHYDRATE 7.3 g of which sugars 7.0 g
FAT 0.1 g of which saturates 0.1 g
FIBRE 0.1 g
SODIUM 0.1 g

Fibre

In a balanced diet, there needs to be a certain amount of fibre from plants. Vegetables, fruit, cereals and brown wholemeal bread all help to keep your digestive system healthy. They provide bulk which helps to move food along.

Carbohydrates

These are rich in energy and come mostly from plants. Bread, potatoes, pasta, rice, flour and sugar are high in energy. If you eat more of these than your body needs, your body will store what it does not need by converting it to fat.

Vitamins

These are found in different foods and you need thirteen different kinds to stay healthy. Vitamin A in carrots is good for your eyes and vitamin C in oranges helps to keep your gums healthy.

Protein

You need protein to keep your body growing and repairing itself, as well as for energy. Protein comes mainly from eating meat, fish, eggs and cheese, and also certain plants such as beans.

Fats

Energy-rich foods and fats are needed for growth of the nervous system and also new cell growth. Although we eat a lot of fat, found in butter, other dairy products and red meat, there is no real need to. Eating large amounts of animal fat can cause heart disease. Fats from plants are thought to be less of a health risk. These fats are in vegetable oils and margarine.

Minerals

These include salt (which you need in tiny amounts), calcium for bones and iron for blood. Calcium comes from milk and you can get iron from spinach.

Teeth

Without teeth, it would be very difficult to eat. You have two sets of teeth. You started to get the first set, your milk teeth, when you were about six months old. You probably lost these when you were about six. The second set gradually grew to replace your milk teeth. You can keep these for the rest of your life, if you look after them. Fortunately, we can go to the dentist if our teeth start to decay. But if you look after your teeth, they should last you a long time.

Some teeth in the second set often grow much later, when you are a teenager or even older. They are called wisdom teeth. Some people get all their wisdom teeth, while others get none.

Teeth grow from inside your jaw and have roots. These roots hold the tooth firmly in the jaw. Your teeth are different shapes and have different jobs to do.

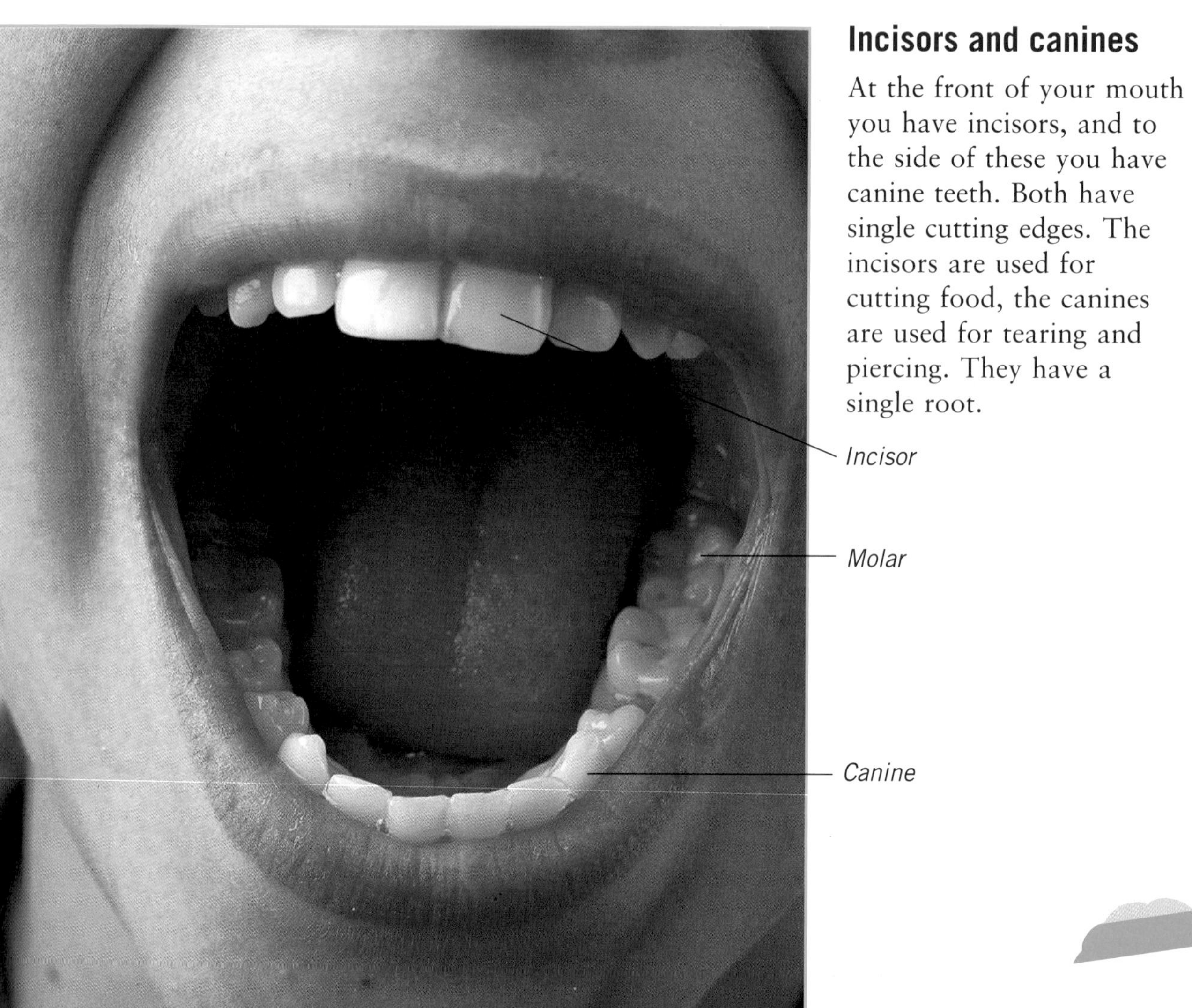

Incisors and canines

At the front of your mouth you have incisors, and to the side of these you have canine teeth. Both have single cutting edges. The incisors are used for cutting food, the canines are used for tearing and piercing. They have a single root.

Premolars and molars

The teeth along your cheek at the back of your mouth are the premolars and the molars. They have a broad surface and are used for chewing and grinding up food. These teeth have two or more roots.

The photo (page 118) shows a molar tooth. The outside of the tooth (above the gum) is covered in a very hard substance called enamel. This is made of minerals – calcium and phosphorous. Most of the rest of the tooth, the part you cannot see because it is in your jaw, is made from hard dentine. Deep inside the tooth is an inner cavity with the pulp. This is the part of the tooth filled with nerves and blood vessels.

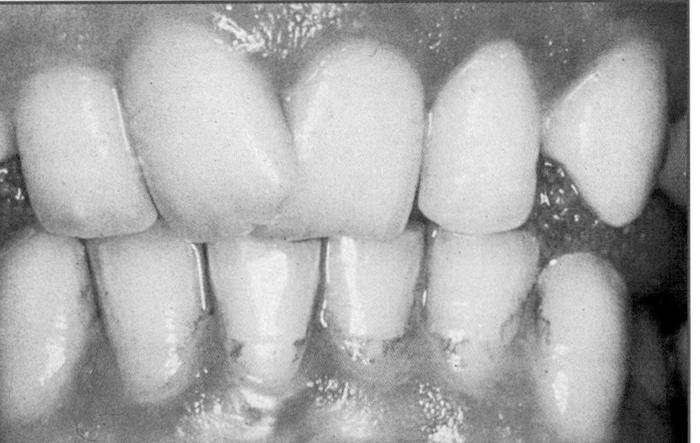

Healthy teeth

Some kinds of food are worse for your teeth than others. Cakes, sweets, biscuits, soft drinks, ice-cream, jam and anything with a lot of sugar in it will stick to your teeth and attract bacteria. This is because the sugar is food for the bacteria that live in your mouth. The bacteria use the sugar but make acid which then eats away at your teeth.

So to make sure you have healthy teeth, always brush them after a meal or eating sweet stuff. When you eat snacks, avoid eating sweets. Try to eat vegetables and fruit such as celery or apples, or even cheese, nuts or corn snacks.

A disclosure test uses red colouring to show plaque on the teeth.

Which teeth?

You can test the design of teeth by biting into an apple with your molars and then try chewing it with your incisors and canines. Also, when you are chewing, watch how your mouth moves. Is it up and down or side to side?

Fascinating fact

In 1979, a Belgian man, John "Hercules" Passis, the man with the strongest teeth in the world, kept a helicopter from taking off by using a mouth harness!

Chew it over

If you are hungry, then you will eat. Food gives you the energy and the chemicals your body needs to keep alive. But every piece of food must change before it can be useful to our bodies. It must be made smaller and smaller until it can be taken into the body.

Teeth and saliva

Teeth, together with saliva (or spit), begin this change. The incisor and the canine teeth cut, bite and tear up pieces of food. Then the molar and premolar teeth along the cheek at the back of the mouth crush and grind up the food (see page 119). Saliva contains a chemical called an enzyme which begins to break down some of the food. Chew a piece of bread and it quickly goes mushy. This happens because, besides grinding the bread with your teeth, there is a chemical reaction which is taking place in your mouth.

Digestion

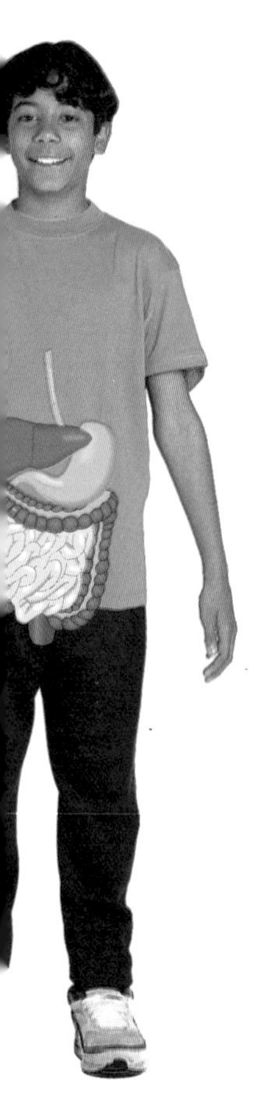

When you swallow your food, it passes down your gullet or oesophagus (1) by a wave-like, muscular action called peristalsis. It enters your stomach (2) where it stays for about three hours. Your stomach twists and turns, and acid and digestive juices break down the food into a thick soup. Digestive juices made by the small intestine (3) and pancreas (4) turn the soup into chemicals small enough for them to pass into your body's blood supply. Small amounts of this soup enter the small intestine where more digestion happens.

The liver (5) produces a green liquid called bile which is stored in the gall bladder (6). Bile helps to break down fats. The wall of the small intestine is folded into millions of tiny 'finger shapes' called villi. This means that as much of the intestine as possible can be covered by the liquid food.

Tiny capillaries of blood lie in the wall of the small intestine and take the chemicals from the food. It is at this point that the food you eat really gets into your body. Up until then, it is just passing through your digestive system, never really becoming part of your body.

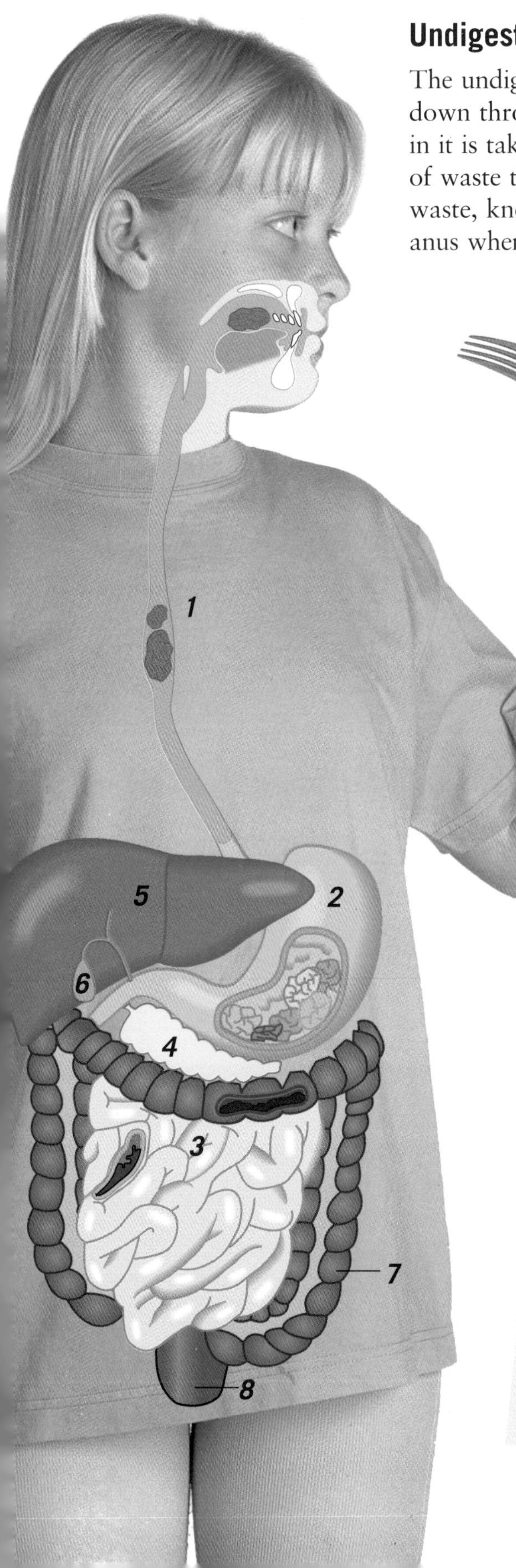

Undigested food

The undigested food which your body cannot use carries down through the large intestine (7), where any water left in it is taken up. So, in the end, all that is left is a dry mass of waste that stays in your rectum (8) for a while. This waste, known as faeces, leaves your body through your anus when you go to the toilet.

Acid in the stomach

Sometimes people eat too much of the wrong kind of food. The stomach may produce too much acid which causes indigestion and a lot of pain. Some people take medicines which act against the acid of the stomach to help stop the pain. Too much acid can lead to stomach ulcers, which can cause the stomach to bleed. Too much of the wrong kinds of food can lead to an unhealthy digestive system.

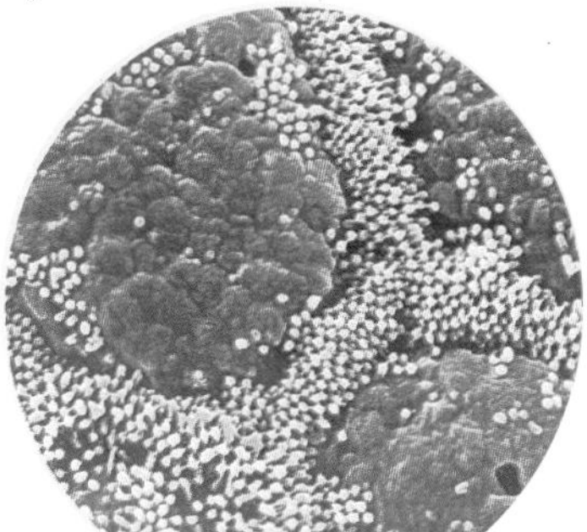

1 2 3 4 5 6 7 8

Food enters the stomach and is broken down by gastric juices.

Mood and food

Sometimes when you have eaten, you may feel that the food seems heavy in your stomach. This may be because of the mood you are in. If you are feeling unhappy, fed up or scared, less digestive juices are made and the food may take sometime to digest. At other times, you may make lots of digestive juices and the food gets digested very quickly.

Staying in balance

Each day of your life, your body is going through changes. Some changes happen quite quickly, such as when you feel hot after running around. Other changes are taking place over a much longer time, such as your growth. Some changes are almost immediate, such as when you are in an emergency and something horrible is about to happen. For example, when you fall off a bicycle, or when you wake up in a cold sweat after a nightmare.

All these things are controlled by tiny amounts of chemicals in your blood called hormones. Hormones are produced by special glands around your body. All these are controlled by the pituitary gland and a part of the brain called the hypothalamus. Hormones help your body get ready for changes whether they happen right away or over a long time.

Hormones are essential for our survival. They control so much in our bodies and they are very powerful because they can make instant changes as well as much longer changes.

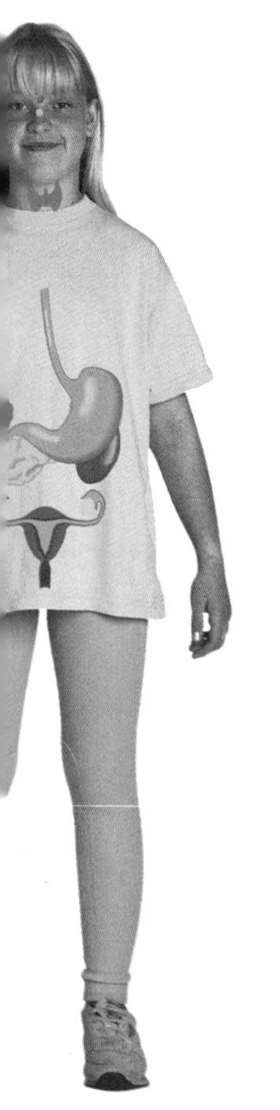

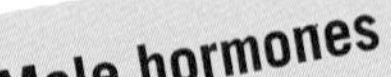

Male hormones
The testes in a man make a hormone which helps control the development of male features such as a beard.

Female hormones
The ovaries in a woman make hormones which control both the development of female features when a girl grows into a woman and also a woman's periods and pregnancy.

The testes produce a hormone called testosterone which brings about the changes from boy to man at puberty (see page 34).

Hormones and glands

The **hypothalamus gland** (1) stimulates the pituitary gland to release hormones.

The **pituitary gland** (2) helps control the balance of water in your body by regulating the amount of water that is removed by your kidneys (see page 16). It also helps to control your growth and makes sure that a woman who has just had a baby makes milk to feed it.

The **thyroid glands** (3) control the way energy from food is released as well as controlling the temperature of your body. They also control the growth of your nervous system. The parathyroids, next to the thyroid glands, control the amount of calcium in your blood and bones.

The **pancreas** (4) makes an important hormone called insulin which controls the amount of sugar in your blood. Some people suffer from a disease called diabetes. This means their pancreas does not make insulin. Sometimes they have to inject themselves with insulin to keep the sugar in their blood at the right level.

The **stomach wall** (5) makes a hormone which turns on the production of acid in the stomach. The small intestine then releases another different hormone which turns the production of acid off. This means that acid is produced only when it is needed.

The **adrenal glands** (6) produce different hormones which help your body cope in an emergency. They also help with water balance, making sure that you have just the right amount of water in your body.

1
2
3
5
6
4
testes

Skin nails and hair

Skin, hair and nails all have one thing in common. They are growing all the time. You have to cut hair and nails but as new skin grows the old, dead skin is just flaking off our bodies. Much of the dust around our home is caused by dead skin. A person one and a half metres tall gives off over 300 grammes of dead skin each year.

You can test for yourself that skin comes off. When you mark your hand with ink from a biro, it is difficult to get off. Watch how long it takes before it disappears. This is the time it takes for your skin to be replaced. Skin flaking off is the natural way for the germs and diseases which land on your body to be removed. But also, as you grow, new skin needs to be made. So your skin keeps growing and the old skin just flakes off all through your life.

What is skin?

Skin may look simple but a closer look shows that it is quite a complicated structure. The top layer is the epidermis, which is a dead layer of skin, that protects the body from infection. The layer beneath this is the dermis which is the living part of the skin. Here, there are hair follicles from which hair grows. Then there are oil glands to make the skin waterproof. There are sweat glands which produce sweat when our bodies get hot.

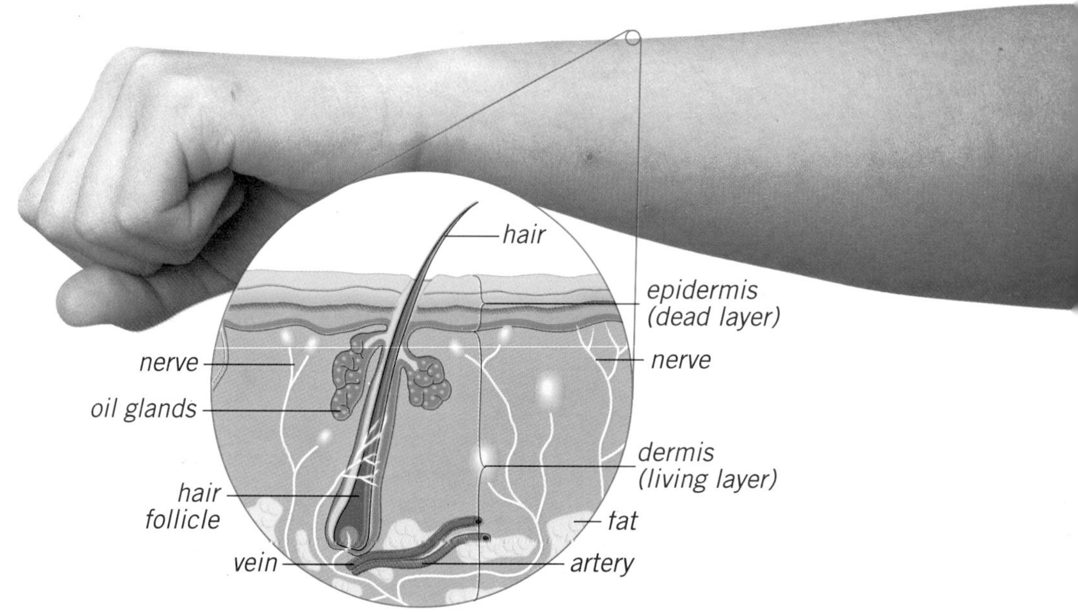

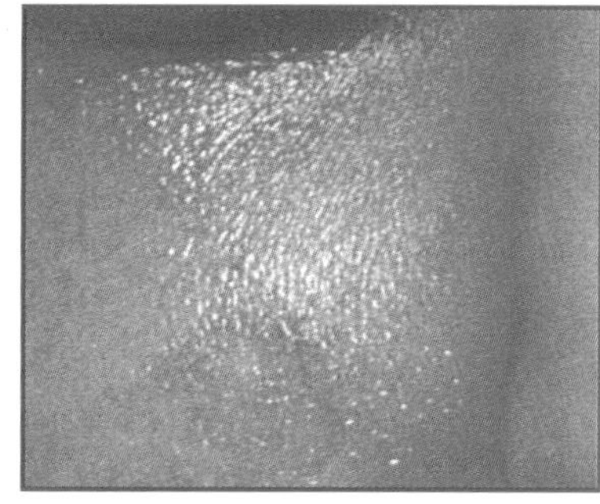

When we get hot, more blood vessels open up and blood flows closer to the skin so heat can escape. The hairs flop down and the sweat glands make sweat to help keep us cool. When we are cold, the blood vessels close down so heat cannot escape easily through our skin. At the same time, the hairs stick up and trap air between the skin and the cold air. This makes an insulating layer of warm air. If we were hairy all over, this would help us to stay warm. But because we do not have much hair, the empty hair follicles stand up on our skin and appear as goose pimples.

Sweat (above) helps us keep cool. Goose pimples appear when we are very cold.

Growing hair and nails

Hair and nails are made out of the same kind of stuff called keratin. Hairs grow, are shed, and then replaced by a new one growing underneath. Hair needs washing as the dried skin from our heads can create unpleasant dandruff.

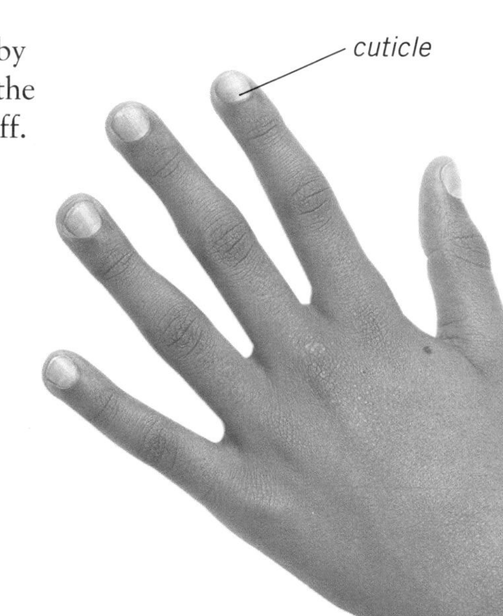

Nails grow from skin that lies under the cuticle, the white half moon shape at the bottom of the nail. They grow all the time and need to be cut.

Caring for your skin

Although our body sheds skin to help keep clean, we need to wash regularly. Bacteria quickly grow on sweat and make it smelly. If we did not wash our skin, we would become very smelly, and not very popular with other people!

Skin cancer

Skin can suffer from a disease called skin cancer. This can happen when your skin gets burnt by the sun. People with dark skin are at less risk than people with fair skin. This is because dark skinned people have more melanin in their skin than people with light coloured skin. Melanin is a pigment (substance) which protects skin from sunburn. To reduce the risk of getting skin cancer, it is a good idea to use high protection sun creams which stop skin from burning when you are in the sun.

Fighting diseases

Although skin can help to keep out germs that can cause disease, your body needs other, more powerful ways to deal with these invaders. This is because, from the day that you were born, all kinds of other living things get inside your body and can make you unwell. These include bacteria, viruses and even bigger living things called parasites. They are all around and our body has to fight them off.

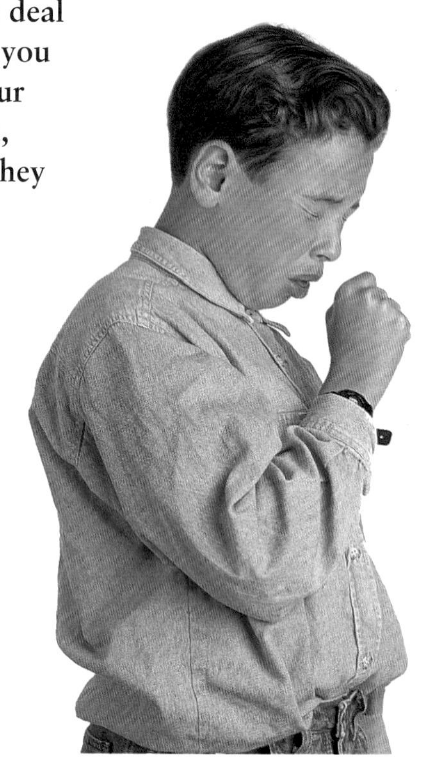

Bacteria

Bacteria are everywhere, even living inside our digestive system. You can only see them through a microscope as they are so tiny. Some are harmful and if we swallow them, through eating bad food or drinking unsafe water or by cutting our skin, they get into the body. They spread very quickly and make us unwell. Bacteria cause diseases such as tonsilitis and some food poisoning. When a cut on your skin turns messy, you get yellow, sticky stuff around it called pus. That is caused by bacteria getting into the cut.

Viruses

Viruses are smaller than bacteria and they invade the living material in a cell, taking it over and using it to grow. Viruses can spread quickly through our bodies and cause diseases such as colds and flu, measles and chicken-pox. Many of the illnesses caused by both bacteria and viruses can be passed on to anothers through coughing and sneezing. When this happens, we say that the disease is infectious.

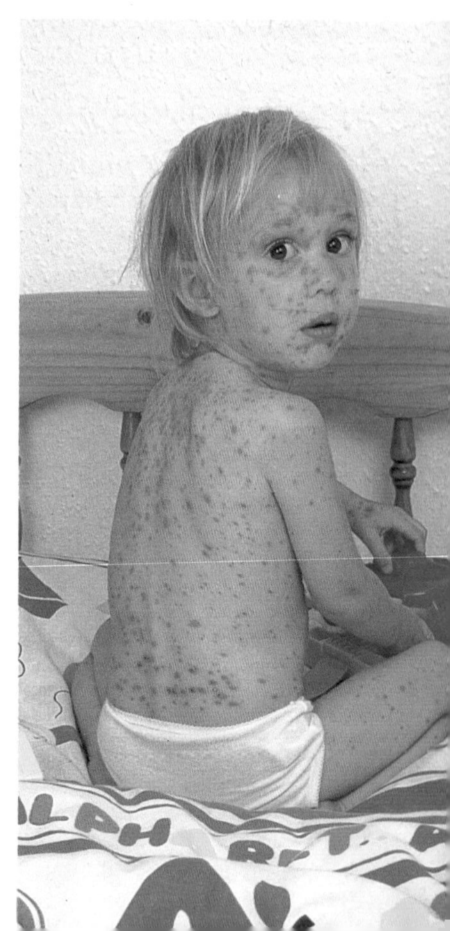

Chicken-pox is a mild infectious disease with an itchy rash and slight fever.

Antibodies

Your body fights infections and diseases through the lymphatic system. This is made up of vessels in your body connected to small swellings called lymph nodes. Special kinds of white blood cells, called lymphocytes, are made in these nodes. They make chemicals called antibodies which get into the blood when an invading germ enters your body. Each different germ causes a different antibody to be made. The antibody will help fight off the disease. When that germ appears again in your body, the antibody can be made very quickly. It can get rid of the germ much more easily, because it has made it once before. Knowing this has helped people to fight disease by using vaccination.

Vaccination

Vaccination works by injecting tiny amounts of dead or harmless germs into a healthy body, which will then make antibodies. Should the dangerous germs get into your body, the antibodies will be made very quickly. They will be able to defend the body and fight off the germs more easily. Being vaccinated helps you fight off the disease. Killer diseases such as polio and smallpox have been controlled through vaccinating people. Viruses are changing all the time and adapting to medicines. This means the human body will always have to fight off diseases.

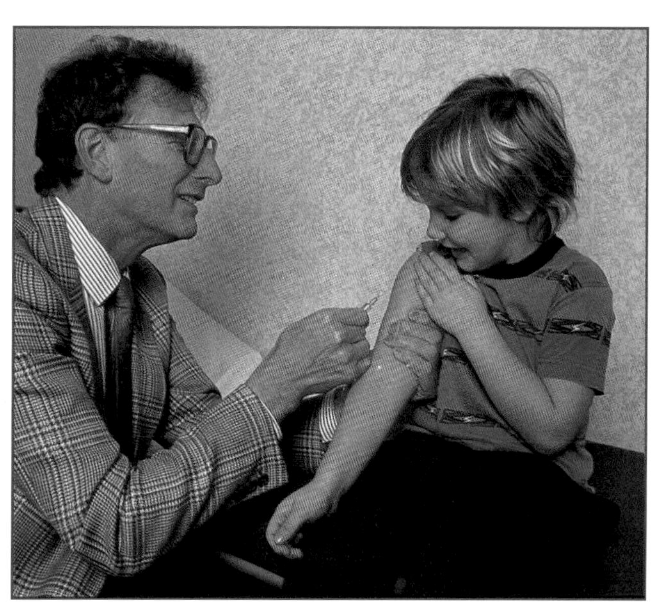

Vaccination helps to reduce the risk of serious illness.

Hygiene

You can reduce the chances of getting diseases by making sure you wash your hands after going to the toilet, and before eating your food. Germs pass easily from the environment into your mouth so basic hygiene can help to make sure you do not get infected. People who handle food have to be particularly careful. They can easily pass on any infection they may carry to other people eating the food they have handled.

People are reminded to wash their hands, especially in food preparation areas.

Growing and changing

Even when you are asleep, your body keeps working all the time. It is also active in other ways, such as when you are growing. These changes take place most quickly when you are young. After birth, babies grow very quickly and they begin to explore, discover and find out about their environment.

As we grow, we experience and learn many different things which helps us survive. Eventually, we come to know about the world we live in. Not only does our knowledge grow, but we grow taller and the shape of our body changes as we grow.

Baby to child

A baby's face has a much smaller chin and nose than an adult, and very rounded cheeks and forehead. The baby's looks gradually disappear as a child grows.

Puberty

Between the ages of 10 and 14 years for a girl and 12 to 15 years for a boy, the next big change happens. This is called puberty where the body is getting ready to have children.

There is no right or wrong time for puberty. Everyone gets there in the end. Quite quickly, boys and girls begin the changes which will make them look and be more like adults. They can do things that adults can do but they still have to learn and experience different things about their bodies, themselves and the way they feel. They are no longer children. This new way of looking and being in the world means there are new things to learn about themselves and others who are growing around them.

Being an adult

At eighteen, they are an adult and their bodies are fully developed. Often this is the age when many people want to become more independent of their parents. They might even move away from home to take responsibility for their own life, without relying so heavily on their parents.

Growing older

The human body stops growing at around the age of twenty years. From that point on, our bodies are gradually slowing down. At about the age of fifty, the body begins to change again, although gradually. So the hair may become grey, muscles become weaker and the skin becomes looser and more wrinkled.

Women are not able to have babies any more because they no longer make the eggs they need to do so. From about the age of fifty, women begin a process called the menopause, when they stop having periods (see page 133).

When old age is reached, people may move more slowly, their bones become brittle and they are not so active. Yet these days, people are living longer than ever before. Many more are able to maintain a very active life at what used to be thought old age. Also, more people than before are now living to be a hundred years old.

Knowing your body – boys

As you grow, you will discover changes happening to your own body. These changes are completely normal and show you that you are becoming a man. Don't worry if they happen to you before or after other boys of your age. Nobody is exactly the same. This time of your life is known as puberty and here are some of the changes you will notice.

Changes to your body

Your voice will go croaky and sometimes sound strange. This is because your voice box is getting larger and your voice is 'breaking', making it sound deeper.

On your body you will see thick hair growing under your arms and wiry hair around your penis and testicles. The wiry hair growing around your penis is called pubic hair. You will also find hair growing on your face and you may also notice that you get spots too. Some people may have hair growing on their chest, legs and back. You may notice you are getting taller and your body is changing shape.

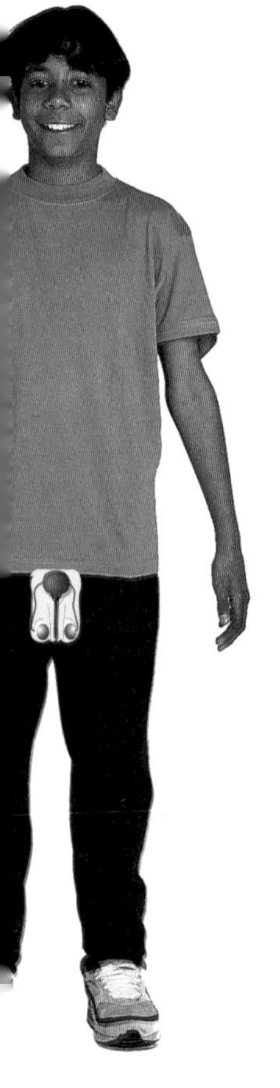

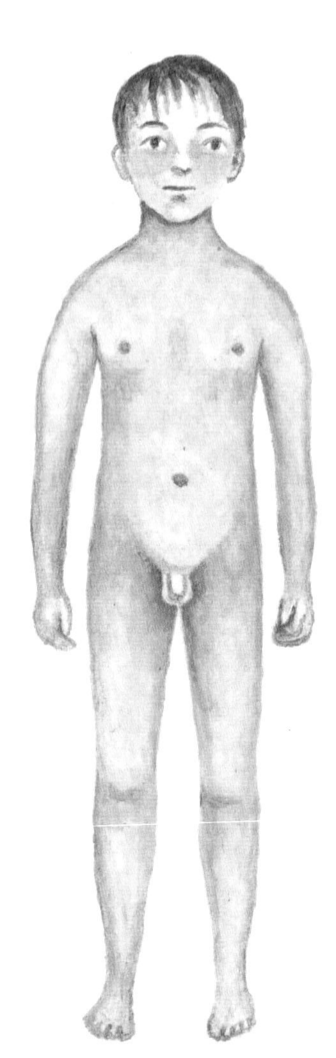

Ejaculation

Your penis grows but it also gets bigger and stiffer very quickly, particularly if you stroke or touch it. This is called getting an erection and happens because blood is pumped into the veins in your penis. When sticky, white liquid squirts out of your penis, this is called ejaculating. It may happen sometimes at night when you are asleep, and take you by surprise. This is known as a wet dream and happens because your body is still getting used to becoming an adult. The white sticky liquid is called semen. It contains seminal fluid and the sperm which you need to help a woman make a baby.

Male sex organs

The picture shows a penis and a pair of testicles. The penis is covered with a foreskin. When a penis is erect, the foreskin is pushed back to show the glans which feels sensitive to the touch. Some people have the foreskin removed for religious or health reasons. White creamy stuff called smegma is made under the foreskin and this helps it move more easily over the glans. When you have passed puberty, it is important to regularly wash stale smegma off your glans.

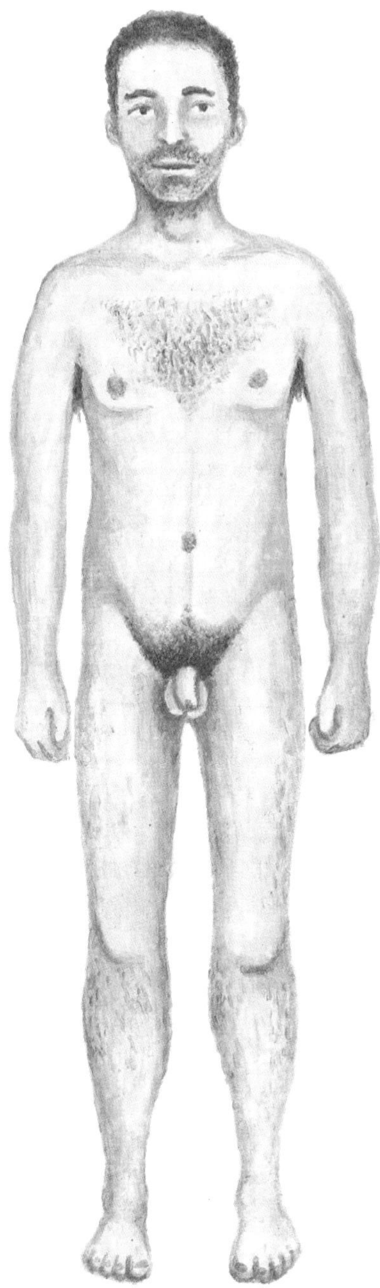

The testicles are made up of the scrotum (the loose bag of skin which holds two testes). The testes make the sperm, and the sperm pass along tubes which join the urethra (see page 134). Urine passes down this tube, as well as semen, but the two never mix. In each ejaculation there is about a teaspoonful of semen which contains around 300 million sperm.

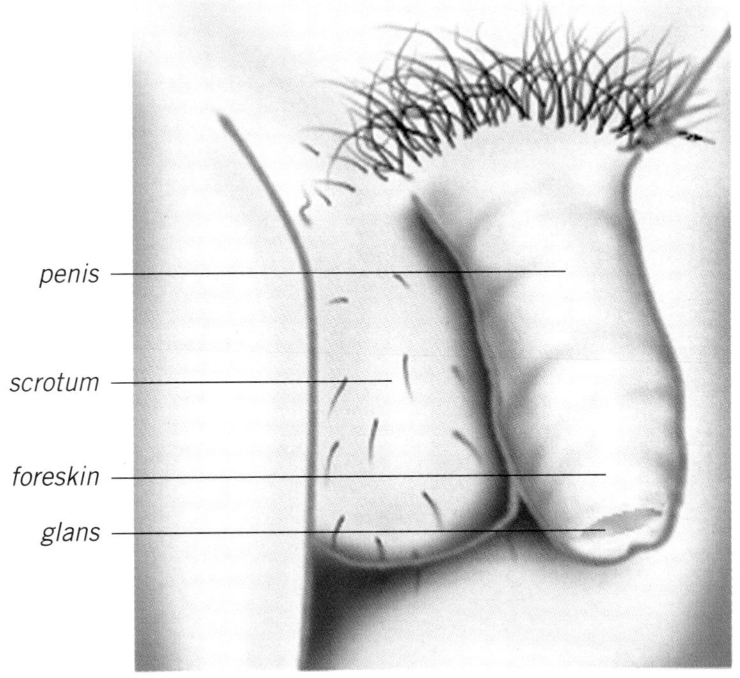

Knowing your body – girls

From about the age of ten to eighteen, girls will go through some very big changes in their bodies. This time of change is known as puberty. It is your body getting itself ready to have babies. For some, the changes happen early; for others, much later. It really does not matter at what time these changes happen, but they will always happen eventually.

Changes to your body

You may first notice thick hair growing under your arms, and wiry hair growing around your vagina area. This wiry hair is called pubic hair. Your breasts begin to grow bigger and become special glands. After having a baby, these glands will make milk to feed the baby. Your hips grow wider so that a baby has room to grow inside the womb. You will start to bleed from the vagina. When this happens it is called having a period.

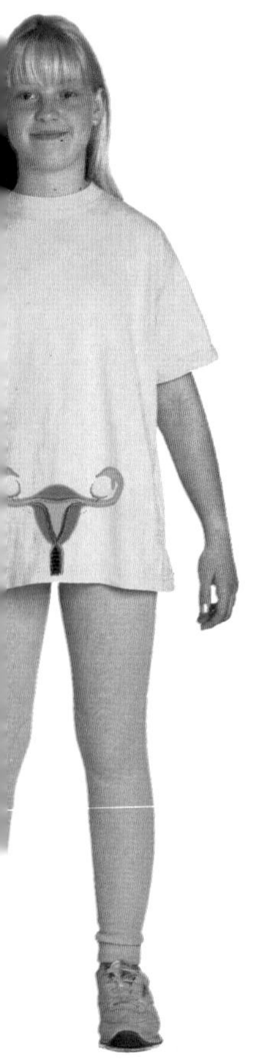

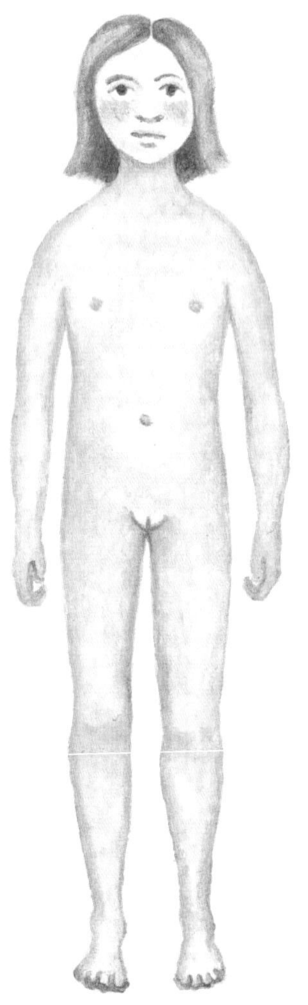

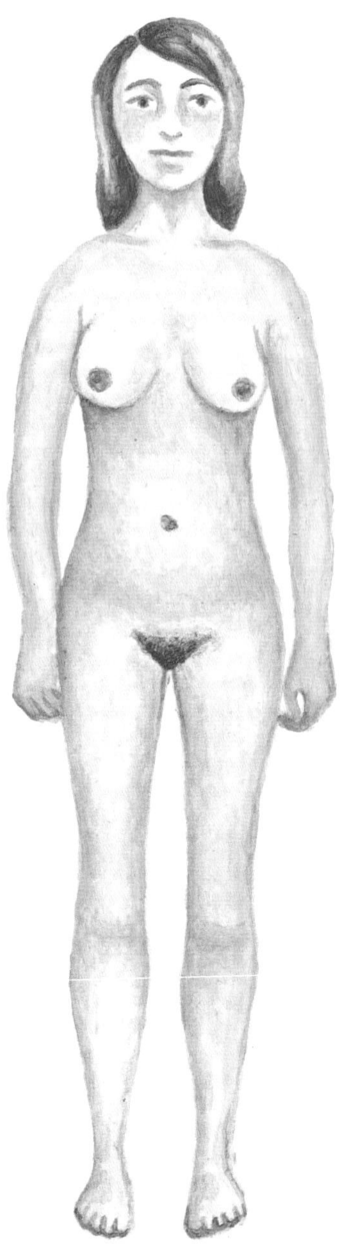

Periods

When you start to have periods they may not be regular. After a time, they will happen once every 20 to 36 days and will last from two to six days. A period is the first few days of the menstrual cycle. About fourteen days after the period starts, an egg is released by an ovary (1) and passes down a fallopian tube (see page 134). Meanwhile, the lining of the uterus (the womb) has become filled with blood and ready to receive a fertilized egg (2). (A fertilized egg is an egg which has joined with a sperm.) If the egg is unfertilized, the uterus lining and the blood come away and pass out through the vagina. This is a period (3)

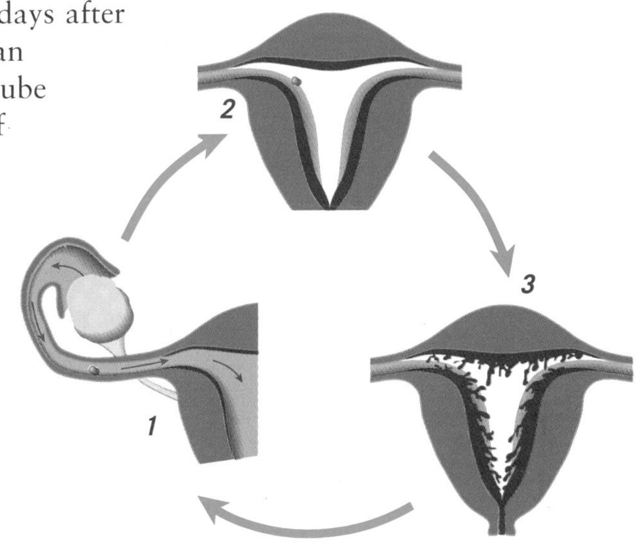

Female sex organs

The picture shows the female sex organs between your legs. The vagina is part of these organs. It is the way out for the blood from a period. It is also where a baby comes out. It is where a man's penis fits, and the way in for sperm to reach an egg. Across part of the opening to the vagina is a thin layer of skin called the hymen. This may break as you grow, or it is harmlessly broken during first sexual intercourse.

Above the vagina is the urinary opening which is connected to your bladder. This is where urine comes out. Above this is the clitoris which is sensitive to touch and helps to make you feel good during sex. Two pairs of skin flaps cover all of these openings. On the outside are the thicker, outer labia or 'lips'. These protect the inner labia underneath. The inner lips are more sensitive. All these structures together make up the vulva.

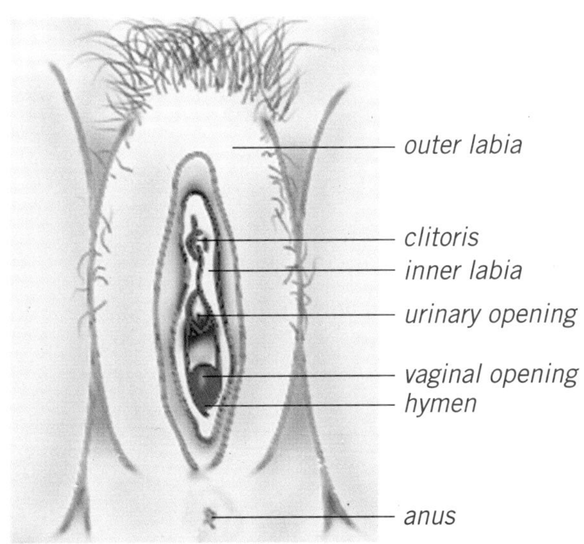

Sex and reproduction

Sex is something most animal life has to do to make more of their own kind. In other words, to have babies. It happens when a sperm meets an egg. For human beings, the sperm has to get from the man's testicles into the woman's vagina, near the neck of the womb (uterus). This happens during sexual intercourse.

During sexual intercourse, the man and the woman want to be very close. Being close in this way is exciting for both. The man's penis becomes erect, and the woman's vagina gets larger and slippery. When they are both ready, the man puts his penis inside the woman's vagina. Both the man and the woman enjoy sexual intercourse because often they each experience something known as an orgasm. An orgasm makes them feel good all over. The woman gets her orgasm through her clitoris, and the man through his penis when he ejaculates (releases sperm).

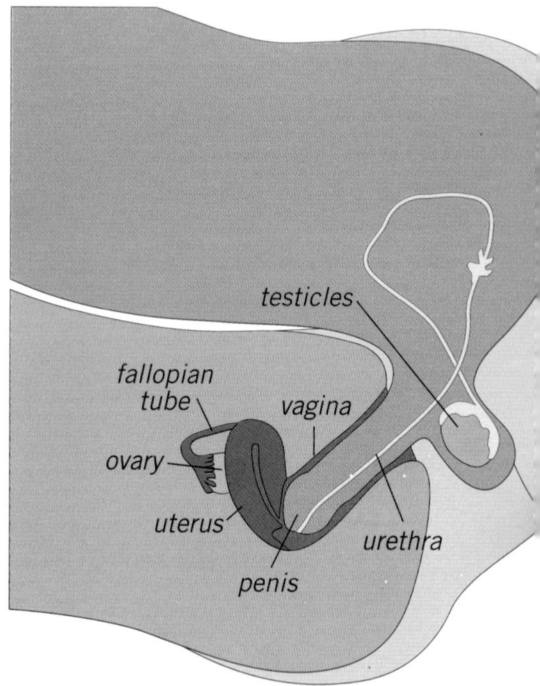

The sperm and the egg

Once inside the vagina, around 300 million sperm begin to swim up into the uterus to find the egg. Each sperm has a head and a tail, and it swims by using its tail. A few hundred sperm cells will reach the egg which is in the fallopian tube, but only one will fertilize the egg to start a new human being. The fertilized egg then passes down the fallopian tube, ready to attach itself to the uterus wall.

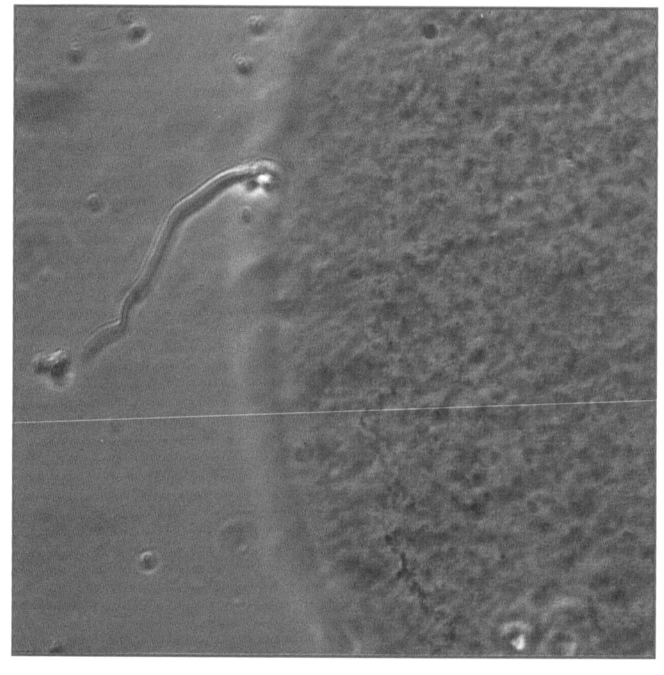

Once a sperm has penetrated the egg wall, no other sperm can reach the egg.

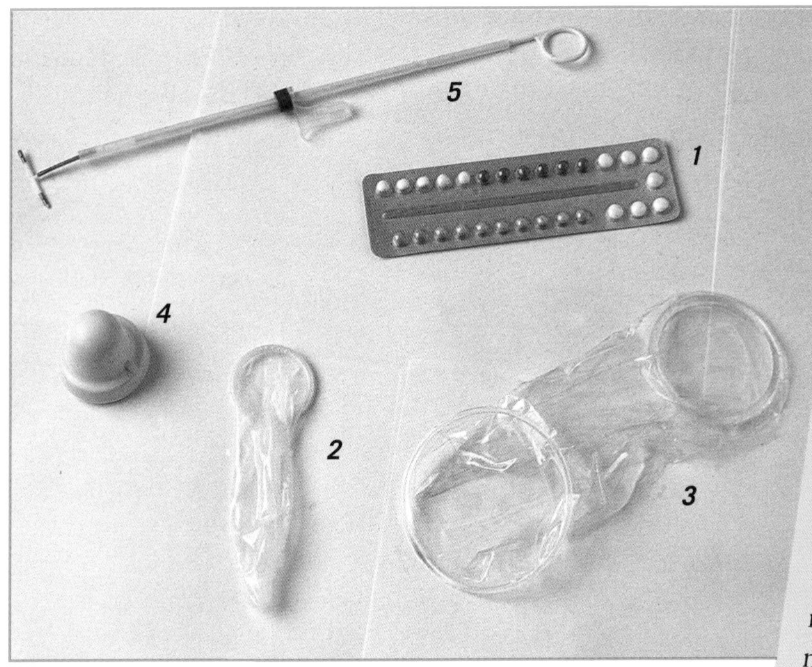

Disease

It is possible for one person to pass on diseases to another as a result of sexual intercourse. These are called Sexually Transmitted Diseases and most can be treated by a doctor. Some diseases, such as AIDS, cannot be cured. When a man uses a condom, it lowers the risk of passing on any disease. Using a condom makes sexual intercourse much safer.

Contraception

Some people have sexual intercourse even though they do not want to have babies. So they may use different ways to stop them from having babies. This is called contraception. Not everybody wants to use contraception because of religious or other reasons. There are several different kinds of contraceptive including:

The pill (1) – a chemical contraceptive taken by women that stops them making any eggs. When the man's sperm get inside her, there are no eggs there for them to fertilize.

The condom or sheath (2) – used mostly by men. This is a barrier contraceptive, because it acts as a barrier to the sperm. The man slides it over his penis, and the sperm are caught inside the condom, never going into the woman at all. There is also a female condom which is inserted just inside the woman's vagina (3).

The cap (4) – another barrier contraceptive used by the woman. She puts it inside her at the top of the vagina on the neck of the womb (the cervix). It blocks the path of the sperm even though they are in the vagina. The cap is covered with spermicide cream, a chemical that kills sperm which slip through.

The coil (5) – has to be fitted by a doctor and it stays at the top of a woman's vagina. Nobody is quite sure how the coil stops women from becoming pregnant.

All contraceptives work by stopping the sperm and the egg meeting.

Choosing a contraceptive that suits a man and woman needs thought. Some methods are better at stopping babies, such as the pill, but because chemicals are being put into the woman's body there are some risks to her health.

Pregnancy and having a baby

When an egg has been fertilized by a sperm, it is ready to attach itself to the inside of the uterus or womb. Each month, since puberty, the uterus has been prepared for this moment. Whilst the new life is growing, the uterus lining will stay in place and help it to develop. The woman will have no more periods whilst the new life grows inside, because the uterus lining stays in place to help the fertilized egg develop.

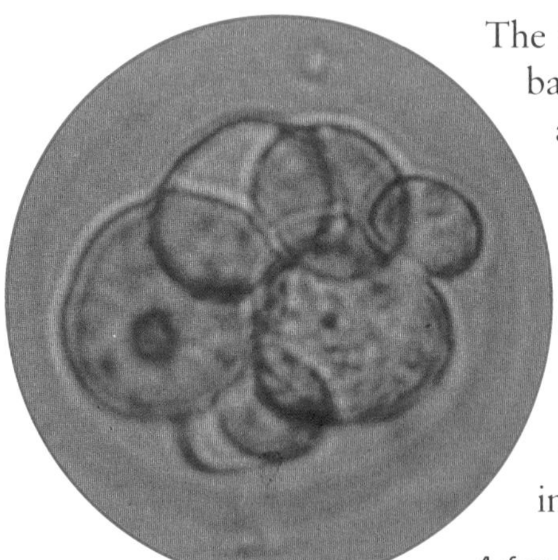

The fertilised egg will divide and divide again, forming a ball of cells. This ball will eventually grow into the baby, and is fixed to the uterus where the placenta grows. The placenta is important to the baby because it is the link between the baby's blood and the mother's blood. The baby's blood and the mother's blood don't mix: they simply exchange things. The baby is connected to the placenta through its umbilical cord and all the mother's food and oxygen passes into the baby along this cord. All the waste that a baby makes passes back into the mother's blood supply through it too.

A few days after conception and the new life is a ball of cells.

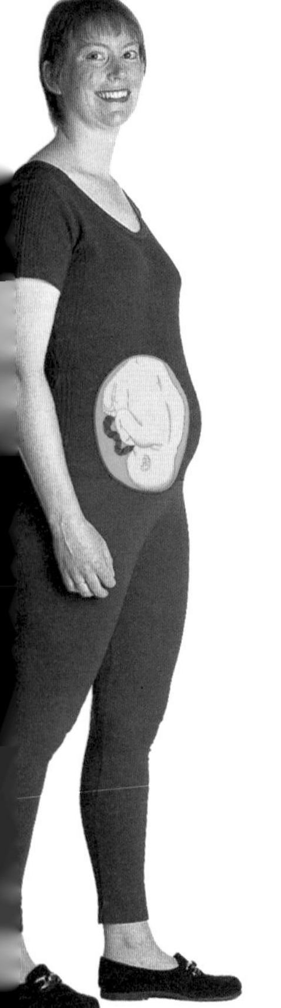

The baby is surrounded by a special sac filled with a liquid called amniotic fluid. This helps to cushion the baby from bumps and sudden movements. The baby remains here for up to nine months growing inside the mother. As it grows, it goes through big changes.

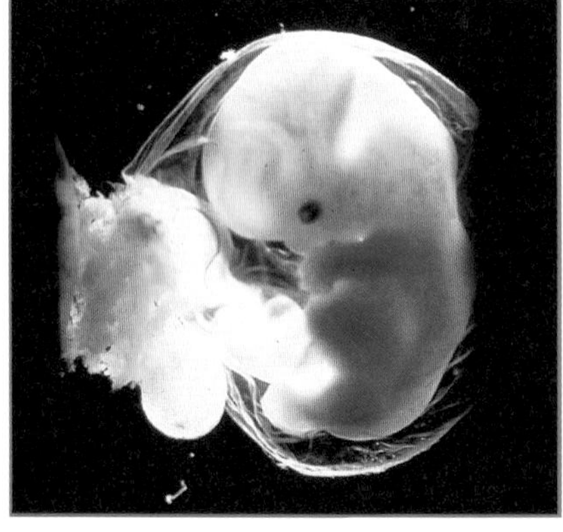

Six weeks pregnant. The baby's heart starts to beat for the first time. All internal organs have begun to form.

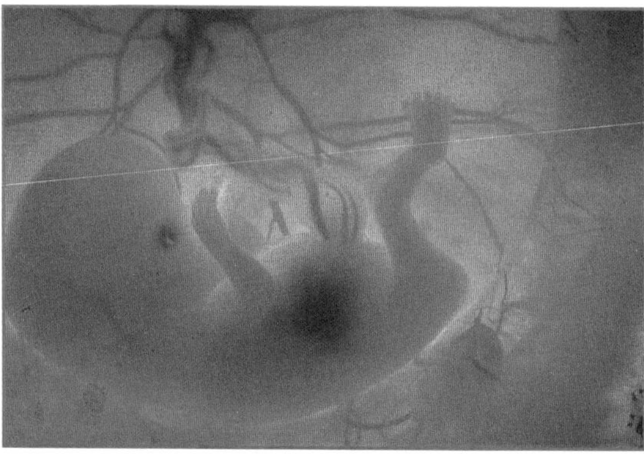

By 12 weeks all the baby's brain, heart and other organs have formed. It weighs 18 grams and is about 6.5 cm long.

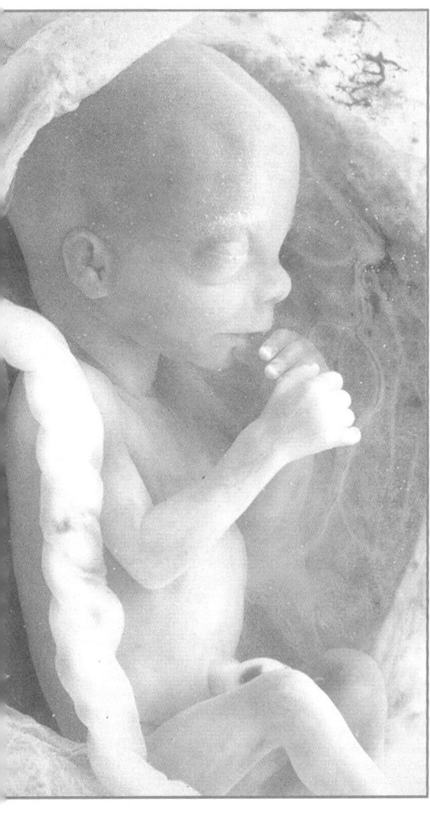

At 26 weeks, the baby has been moving around and the mother regularly feels the baby kicking. It is 30 cm long.

At around 40 weeks, the baby is ready to be born.

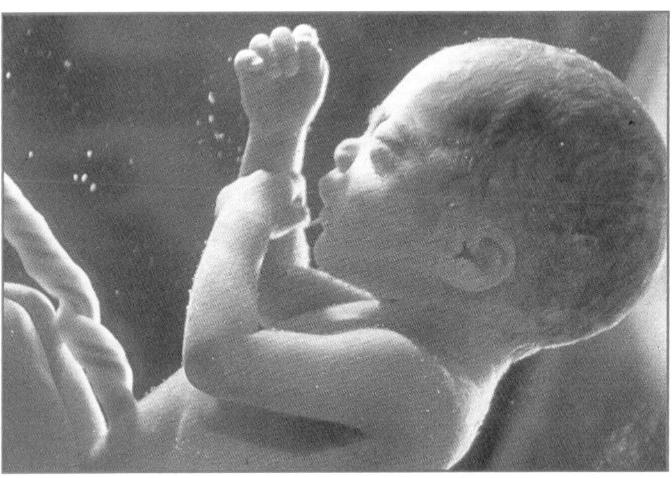

Being born

Shortly before birth, the neck of the womb or cervix slowly opens up and the walls of the womb push the baby down out through the mother's vagina. When the baby comes out, it takes its first breath and cries. It is still connected to the inside of the mother through its umbilical cord. This is cut and tied off. Our tummy button is the scar that is left after we have had our umbilical cord cut. The placenta comes out of the mother a little later after the baby, and so it is often called the afterbirth.

The mother is ready to feed the baby as her breasts begin to make milk for the baby to feed on.

At the first feed, the mother's antibodies, which help to fight disease, are passed to the baby.

Taking responsibility

Part of growing up is thinking for yourself and working out how you want to do things. As you grow older, your parents realise that you no longer want to be told what to do and how to do it. They will give you more freedom to choose for yourself. And you will want to do things your own way.

But with this greater freedom comes a greater sense of responsibility. If you do things your way and they go wrong, you will have to take the blame! Everyone has to learn by making mistakes, even adults. That is just part of learning.

When you are young, you will probably make more mistakes than when you are older. As you grow up, you will realise that only one person can take responsibility for your body and keeping it healthy – you! Only you can know what you are putting into your body and whether it will do you harm. Even if you do something because everyone else is doing it, this does not make it right.

So caring for your body is your responsibility. Here are some things you need to be responsible about. Your body depends on it.

'Drink and drive' warnings

Alcohol

You need to know that alcohol is a drug. Like any drug, it can change the way you feel and can change the way you behave. Quite small amounts can slow down your reactions. When people drink alcohol and then drive a car or other vehicle, they risk their own lives and the lives of others. This is because they are unable to properly judge what is happening around them. Also, many people become violent and may hurt others for no reason. Every day, people are hurt or killed because someone has drunk too much alcohol. Too much alcohol can also lead to kidney and liver failure.

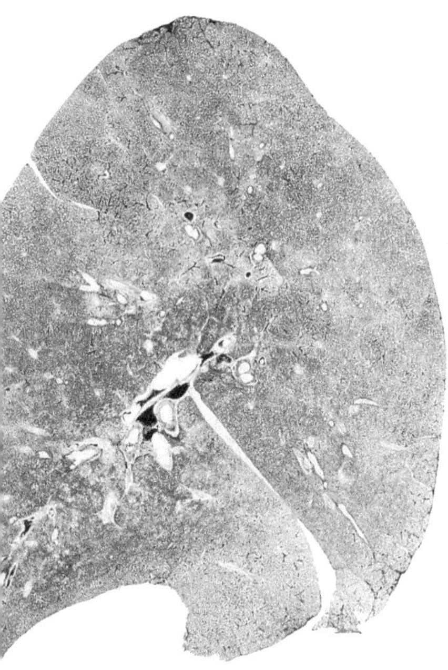

Smoking

Cigarettes, cigars and pipe tobacco contain a drug called nicotine, together with lots of other chemicals. They can cause a disease called cancer. They also cause the lungs to slow down the way they work and the lungs become full of dirt and tar. Smoking cigarettes also increases your chances of getting lung and heart diseases. Most people now agree that smoking is very unhealthy.

A healthy lung

This lung shows patches of tar caused by cigarette smoke.

Drugs

These include marijuana, tablets such as ecstasy and LSD, and hard drugs such as heroin and cocaine. All these drugs change the way people behave. Some, such as the hard drugs, are very addictive and some people turn into addicts. These are people who need to take drugs just to be able to live their life. They find it very difficult to give up because their body has become so used to having the drug. Taking drugs is very dangerous to the health of your mind and body.

All these substances in some form or another are poisons in your body. Your body has to battle against these chemicals each time they enter it. Only you can be responsible for the health of your body.

Exercise

Exercise is particularly important these days. A lot of people spend longer resting than being active. We sit in front of computers or watch television, or even just watch others play sport without playing any ourselves. Taking regular exercise tones the body and helps to keep it healthy.

Exercise helps your body in the following ways:

- It builds up your stamina which means you can do all the other things in your life better and more easily. Even getting down to doing your homework can be improved by having a good level of stamina!

- It makes your heart stronger which gets your circulation working well. Good circulation means that oxygen gets to all the parts of your body.

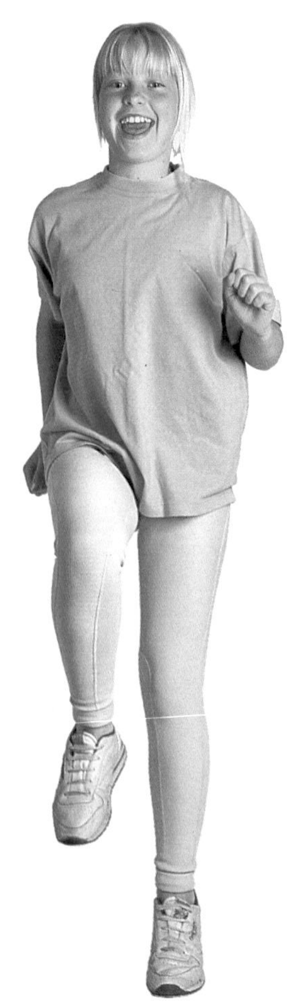

- It makes your lung capacity bigger which means you can breathe in more oxygen and get rid of carbon dioxide more efficiently.

- It helps to keep your weight down because your body uses up more energy and stores less of the food you eat as fat.

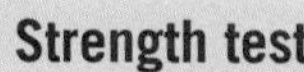

Strength test

Take some ordinary bathroom scales and squeeze them as hard as you can. Make a note of the reading. By exercising your arms and hands, you may be able to make your grip stronger. Using the same scales, test your leg strength. Ask someone to hold the scales against the wall and then, lying on your back, you press your feet against the scales as hard as you can. The person holding the scales can take the reading for you.

- It stimulates your brain to make natural body drugs. Some of these are called endorphins and they leave you with a sense of feeling good and feeling happy.

- It strengthens your muscles so you are able to do all kinds of tasks more easily. It strengthens your joints and makes the muscles in your body supple.

Safety warning

Anyone who hasn't exercised for a while should start gently and gradually build up the level of exercise.

So exercise is important for everyone's health. Whilst at school, periods of strenuous exercise through playing games will help. It is now recommended that you need five 30 minute sessions of exercise a week. Playing sports such as tennis, running, going swimming or cycling all help to keep your body working at peak performance. You do not have to do sport every day, but getting into a habit of doing some strenuous exercise is a good way of making sure that you stay healthy.

Health test

You can test your fitness by measuring your pulse rate before and after taking exercise. To find your pulse rate, feel your pulse for 30 seconds, then double the number. Take your pulse at rest. Then take exercise such as stepping up and down on a step for a couple of minutes. Now take your pulse again. See how long it takes to get back to your resting level. This is a rough measure of how fit you are. The quicker you take to get back to your resting pulse rate, the fitter you are.

Published by BBC Educational Publishing, a division of BBC Education, BBC White City, 201 Wood Lane, London W12 7TS

First published in this form 1997

Colour reproduction by Dot Gradations Ltd, England

Illustrations: © Salvatore Tomaselli 1996 (pages 98-102, 104, 106-108, 110-113, 120-124, 126, 130-134 and 136); © Claire Bushe 1996 (pages 114, 115 and 130-132)

Photos: Ardea/P. Morris **p. 104 (right);** BBC/Luke Finn **135 (left);** BBC/Lesley Howling **p. 125 (top and bottom), 128 (middle right);** Gibbs Oral Hygiene **p. 119 (top and bottom);** Robert Harding Picture Library/Delimage p. 137 (bottom); Image Bank/Steve Allen **p. 137 (top left);** Courtesy of the Kidney Foundation, Midlands **p. 113;** Published by the Portman Group **p. 138 (middle and right);** Rex Features, London **p. 139 (bottom);** Science Photo Library/Alex Bartel **p. 126 (bottom);** Science Photo Library/John Bavosi **p. 105 (left);** Science Photo Library/CNRI **p. 121 (right);** Science Photo Library/Ken Eward **p. 111;** Science Photo Library/Matt Meadows/Peter Arnold Inc **p. 105 (right);** Science Photo Library/Petit Format/JD Bauple **p. 103 (top);** Science Photo Library/Petit Format/CSI **p. 136 (top);** Science Photo Library/Petit Format/Nestle **pp. 136 (bottom), 136 (middle right), 137 (top right);** Science Photo Library/Richard Rawlins **p. 134 (right);** Science Photo Library/Jim Selby **p. 127;** James Steveson **p. 139 (top left and right);** Telegraph Colour Library **p. 129 (left);** Telegraph Colour Library **p. 128 (far left);** Wellcome Institute Library, London **pp. 108-9;** Zefa Pictures UK **pp. 128 (middle left), 129 (middle), 129 (right)**

All other photographs: BBC/Simon Pugh

Cover photos: Tony Stone Images/Charles Krebs (main picture); Telegraph Colour Library/Bildagentur and Bruce Coleman Ltd/Kim Taylor (inset pictures)

Grateful thanks to Jane Goodman and Eastman Dental Hospital, London.

Index

Index